Legal Cleanup

For *NEW JERSEYANS:*

HOW TO EXPUNGE

YOUR CRIMINAL OR JUVENILE RECORD

IN NEW JERSEY, FIRST EDITION

Legal Cleanup

For *NEW JERSEYANS:*

HOW TO EXPUNGE

YOUR CRIMINAL OR JUVENILE RECORD

IN NEW JERSEY, FIRST EDITION

VONNIE DONES III

ATTORNEY-AT-LAW

Dones House

Publishing

Legal Cleanup For New Jerseyans: How To Expunge Your Criminal Or Juvenile Record In New Jersey, First Edition

Disclaimer

Dones House Publishing
200 East 32nd Street
Houston, Texas 77018

TABLE OF CONTENTS

Chapter 3

CLASSIFICATION OF OFFENSES 70

Chapter 4

MULTIPLE CONVICTIONS 140

Chapter 5

DIVERSION / SUPERVISORY TREATMENT PROGRAMS .. 146

Chapter 6

POST-EXPUNGEMENT 166

Chapter 7

EXPUNGEMENT SERVICES AT LEGALCLEANUP.COM 184

BIBLIOGRAPHY 212

APPENDICES

INTRODUCTION

INTRODUCTION

The idea that you can work hard and achieve your dreams of going to college, getting a good job, and raising a family is the cornerstone of American society. Unfortunately, the economic and social consequences of having a criminal record in today's society can stand in the way of your dreams and negatively impact your life forever. A conviction or an arrest for a criminal or misdemeanor offense means that you have a criminal history record that is publicly available for everyone to see. Contrary to popular belief, dismissed or dropped charges or a not guilty verdict by a judge or jury does not mean that you automatically escape the ostracism associated with having a criminal record. You beat the case but not the rep. Unfortunately, anyone who sees your criminal record will unfairly view your innocence with skepticism. The simple solution is to expunge your criminal record and restore your reputation. Otherwise, your criminal record could haunt you for the rest of your life.

The good news is that many states are re-thinking its' expungement laws to help "ex-offenders" get a second chance at life. Fortunately, many states have an interest in helping "ex-offenders" re-integrate into society. In many states, clearing, destroying, erasing, setting aside, isolating, or sealing a criminal record is often referred to as expungement. Although the terms are interchangeably used, the meaning of each term will vary depending on your state. All expunged records are sealed, but not all sealed records are expunged.

Forty-five (45) of Fifty (50) states in the United States and the District of Columbia have laws that allow "ex-offenders" to expunge or seal their criminal record. Nearly

INTRODUCTION

all states permit an expungement or sealing for arrests not resulting in a conviction and misdemeanor convictions. However, some states do not permit expungement or sealing for serious crimes or felonies. The laws regulating expungement eligibility varies by state. Each state has its' own set of criteria to evaluate whether a person deserves a second chance. Generally, the court will deny or grant your petition for expungement or sealing by looking at whether you have any current pending charges, prior or subsequent criminal conviction(s), any serious offenses, satisfied the waiting period requirement(s), and completed the court's sentence. In addition, a majority of states have some type of treatment program to rehabilitate an "ex-offender" to the extent he or she can successfully re-integrate into society.

Today, with criminal background checks being so routinely performed on the internet, it is more important than ever to expunge your criminal record. Leaving your criminal history record exposed to employers, landlords, licensing agencies, or the like, can prevent you from taking advantage of many career or financial opportunities that may come your way. Expungement provides an "ex-offender" a "fresh start" at life. The goal of expungement law is to provide an avenue for "ex-offenders" to rebuild their lives and start anew.

This book specifically discusses expungement law in the State of New Jersey. In New Jersey, the most recent legislative amendments involving expungement law have been in support of making expungement more accessible. The following legislative amendments represent some of the latest changes to expungement law supporting "ex-offender" rehabilitation in New Jersey:

- a shorter waiting period required to expunge statutorily approved indictable offenses;

- no automatic disqualification for expungement if fines are not paid;

- waiting period reduced for juvenile offenders;

- the expungement of certain types of drug distribution convictions; and

- the establishment of the new conditional dismissal program.

Use this book to determine if you are eligible for expungement and whether expungement is the right course of action for you. In addition, you must determine if

INTRODUCTION

you want to represent yourself, hire an attorney to provide limited representation, or hire an attorney to fully represent you. This book outlines the requirements you must satisfy to successfully expunge your criminal record in New Jersey. In addition, this book will help guide you through the process of cleaning up your criminal record without an attorney or with an attorney providing limited representation. Every applicant's situation is different and can vary from basic to complex. Be sure to carefully evaluate the facts and circumstances surrounding your case to determine your best course of action. In New Jersey, you may only get one shot to get it right in most cases, so make it your best shot.

After you have closely reviewed all the requirements for expungement in New Jersey, you must file your petition with the court. A properly prepared petition and a strict adherence to statutory procedure will ultimately lead you to successfully expunging your criminal record. Petitioning the court for expungement is a time-consuming and arduous task. It requires the mailing of several expungement documents to the court(s) and various government agencies. The government agencies that you are legally required to provide notice of your petition will depend on the circumstances of your case. The following factors will determine which government agencies you must legally provide notice when you are applying for expungement in New Jersey:

- Whether you are petitioning the court to expunge a juvenile or adult record.

- Whether you were arrested by more than one police department or agency.

- Whether you have multiple convictions in more than one county.

- Whether you were on parole or probation, enrolled in an adult or juvenile diversion or supervisory treatment program, granted a deferred disposition or performed community service.

- Whether you were processed through a State Grand Jury.

After the court grants your petition for expungement, you should notify private database companies of your expunged criminal record. Note that although you have expunged your criminal record and it is publicly unavailable to anyone doing

INTRODUCTION

an "official search," your record may still be available to those doing an "unofficial search" using a private database company. Therefore, after the court grants your petition for expungement, you should notify private database companies of your expunged record. By law, private database companies must then update their information in a timely fashion to accurately reflect the court's order.

In conclusion, if you have a criminal record in New Jersey and you find that you are eligible, you should apply for an expungement. If you have ever been arrested or charged with an offense, you should check your records for any errors. Your record may list an arrest, but fail to accurately state that the charge against you was ultimately dismissed. An employer seeing this may wrongfully assume your arrest resulted in a conviction. Or, you may have one arrest, but the arrest was incorrectly listed more than once on your record. Clearing your criminal record can save you a lot of headaches and frustration. Many people have expunged their criminal records and are enjoying a new lease on life. Use this book to open up a new world of social and economic opportunities.

CHAPTER 1:
EXPUNGEMENT BASICS 101

S1.

What is an Expungement?

Under New Jersey law, an expungement is an extraction and isolation of records pertaining to one's criminal history. Therefore, expunged criminal records in New Jersey are not "erased," or "destroyed," but segregated and not generally available when someone does an "official search." An "official search" is a search in which one does with a court system or law enforcement. After a judge grants an expungement order, a petitioner will receive a signed court order from the judge stating that the offense "...shall be deemed not to have occurred and the petitioner may answer any questions accordingly." [28] The courts, detention or correctional facilities, law enforcement agencies, and probation departments must remove all expunged records to an isolated location. Thus, all expunged records are no longer publicly available. The general public, employers, insurance companies, landlords, adoption agencies, creditors, or the like performing a background check will not have access to such records. A requestor will receive the message "no record." Expunged records include "complaints, warrants, arrests, commitments, processing records, fingerprints, photographs, index cards, "rap sheets" and judicial docket records." [6]

EXPUNGEMENT BASICS: 101

If I expunge my conviction, can I legally say I have never been arrested?

With some exceptions, once you expunge your arrest(s) and/or conviction(s), you are legally permitted to say under oath that it never occurred. In addition, expunging your criminal record will eliminate all civil disabilities put into effect as a result of your arrest or conviction.

What are some exceptions to legally denying or not having to divulge your expunged criminal record?

You must divulge your record if you are applying for a job with the following government agencies: (N.J.S.A. 2C:52-27(c)); [1]

1.   the court,

2.   a law enforcement agency,

3.   department of corrections, or

4.   the judicial branch of government.

You must divulge your record if requested by the following agencies or in the following situations:

1.   Use of Expunged Records by Holding Agency in a Pending Petition for Expungement, (N.J.S.A. 2C:52-17)

2.   Use of Expunged Records by the Violent Crimes Compensation Board, (N.J.S.A. 2C:52-18)

3.   Inspections of Records by Court Order, (N.J.S.A. 2C:52-19)

4.   Use of Expunged Records for Diversion Program, (N.J.S.A. 2C:52-20)

5.   Use of Expunged Records for Bail Hearing / Presentence Report / Sentencing, (N.J.S.A. 2C:52-21)

6.   Use of Expunged Records by Parole Board, or (N.J.S.A. 2C:52-22)

7.   Use of Expunged Records by Department of Corrections (N.J.S.A. 2C:52-23)

While expungement of your criminal record will prevent employers or the like performing an "official search" from gaining access to your criminal records, it will not prevent private database companies performing an "unofficial search" from sharing your outdated information with requestors, as discussed below.

Can a private database company report a criminal record after expungement?

After your criminal record is expunged, generally within 30-60 days, it will be removed from state and federal databases. Private background check providers may still report your outdated record. Therefore, to ensure that private background check providers do not report your outdated record to employers or the like performing a criminal background check, it is important that you notify private database companies of your expunged or sealed record. After notification, the provider is required to comply with the judge's order of expungement or sealing and remove the outdated information.

Note Before You Continue

Our law firm offers four (4) expungement service packages. With the exception of our Attorney Standard Package, we notify over 500 private database companies of your expunged or sealed record. Generally, the record clearance update is completed within thirty (30) days from such time providers are notified. In this book, we provide you with all the information you will need to notify private database companies of their legal obligation to update your records, once you have expunged your criminal record. See S57.

What is the purpose of an expungement?

The purpose of an expungement is to provide an "ex-offender" who has demonstrated rehabilitation a chance to re-integrate into society. Expunging your criminal record will conceal your records from public view. The intent of the New Jersey State Legislature in enacting expungement legislation is to give deserving "ex-offenders" or "first-time offenders," a "clean start." "Ex-offenders" or "first-time offenders" who have managed to overcome their troubled past and change their lives for the better, deserve an opportunity to fully re-integrate into society. Expunging a criminal record gives a deserving "ex-offender" or "first-time offender" a "clean slate," so that he or she can become a productive member of society. The idea is for "ex-offenders" or "first-time offenders" to receive appropriate penalties without the backlash of a permanent criminal record. In recent years, the New Jersey courts have made significant strides towards providing deserving "ex-offenders," or "first-time offenders," with the chance to re-integrate into society.

However, the New Jersey State Legislature and the New Jersey Courts both recognize that there is a delicate balancing of public policy that persists in expungement law. On one hand, it is important for the New Jersey legislature and courts to give "ex-offenders" or "first-time offenders" who have undergone rehabilitation a chance to re-integrate into society and recapture the American dream. On the other hand, the public's need to access criminal history records for public safety is of equal importance. Therefore, the New Jersey legislature and courts balance the two public policy measures by setting forth requirements for expungement eligibility based on the type of conviction(s), seriousness of the conviction(s), number of convictions, time passed since the conviction(s), and rehabilitative measures taken since the conviction(s).

S2.

Why Expunge Now?

Expunging your criminal record can help you in the following ways:

Employment - Most employers will do a criminal background check before hiring you and will not hire you if you have a criminal record. A criminal record is a serious matter that can prevent you from obtaining employment. If you have ever been arrested, charged with an offense, or convicted of an offense, you have a criminal record. In today's job market, competition for jobs is fierce. There are many qualified applicants competing in a limited job market. Many people are finding it difficult to secure employment in such a market. If you have a criminal record, your chances of obtaining employment are even slimmer. Therefore, if you are eligible for expungement, you should expunge your criminal record immediately! Do not lose out on your dream job simply because you neglected to expunge your criminal record.

Loans - A criminal record will make it more difficult, if not impossible in some cases, for you to obtain a home or auto loan. Many banks or loan agencies will view a criminal record as a credit risk. Loan agencies approve loans based on a set of criteria that reduces the risk of their customers defaulting on their loan. In the eyes of a loan agency, a criminal record signifies a lack of reliability. If you a have a criminal record, a loan agency will often tack on larger premiums or higher interest rates to counter the financial risk of approving such a loan. When completing a loan application, a lender may ask you if you have ever been convicted of a crime. If you have expunged your criminal record, you may legally answer "no" to the question. If you have not, you must answer "yes" and list all of your criminal convictions. Be sure that you are truthful when answering any questions related to your criminal record. There are serious consequences and penalties for being dishonest about your criminal background. Therefore, to avoid scrutiny into your criminal background you should expunge your criminal record.

Financial Aid - Federal student aid is not available for students with certain types of drug or sexual offense convictions. Such convictions may limit your eligibility for federal student aid. Be sure to check with the U.S. Department of Education or federal guidelines to determine your eligibility status. You should note that limited eligibility may not apply to non-federal student aid. Therefore, even if you are ineligible for federal student aid, you should complete the Application for Federal Student Aid (FAFSA), because most schools or states will make a decision on whether to award you any type of financial aid by using the information on your FAFSA. [26]

Leasing / Renting - Some landlords may refuse to rent to a person who has a criminal background. A landlord may legally refuse to rent to a person based on his or her poor credit history, lack of sufficient income to pay rent, bad references from a previous employer or landlord, criminal conviction(s), or prior eviction lawsuit (even if he or she won the lawsuit). [27] As long as a landlord does not discriminate or violate the Federal Fair Housing Acts (42 U.S. Code §§ 3601-3619) which prohibits discrimination on the basis of race, color, religion, national origin, gender, age, familial status (having children), and physical or mental disability, (including alcoholism and past drug addiction) he or she can reject whomever they choose. [27] Do not be forced to live in an unpleasant or high crime area simply because you have neglected to clean your criminal record. Avoid a bad situation for you and your family by simply cleaning your criminal record history. If you have children in school, be proactive, and avoid being zoned to a school in an area that could hinder their chance at a good education.

Business Venture - Many investors or potential business partners perceive a criminal record as a "red flag." Do not ruin your opportunity for a successful business venture by not cleaning the stain on your criminal record.

Adoption- In New Jersey, certain types of convictions on your criminal record can prevent you from adopting a child. See N.J.A.C. 30:4C-26.8(d). A background check will not only be performed on prospective foster parents, but on every household member over the age of 18. See N.J.A.C. 30:4C-26.8(b).

If the prospective resource family parent or any adult residing in the prospective parent's home has a record of criminal history, the Department of Children and Families shall review the record with respect to the type and date of the criminal offense and make a determination as to the suitability of the person to become a resource family parent or the suitability of placing a child in that person's home, as the case may be. See N.J.A.C. 30:4C-26.8b.

Be sure to check N.J.A.C. 10:122C-5.4 and 5.5 to determine whether your offense disqualifies you from adopting a child. [6]; [29] However, if you have a disqualifying offense on your criminal record that is eligible for expungement, you should expunge your criminal record now to heighten your chances of success. See Appendix G, "Adoption, Child Placement, & Investigation," for statutory law on criminal investigations for adoption.

Volunteering - A criminal record may prevent you from volunteering in your community if your volunteer work involves working with children. A criminal record does not disqualify you from volunteering in all cases. However, it may prevent you from acting as a little league coach, attending overnight youth camps, or working one-on-one with children. You should expunge your criminal record if you find that you are eligible for expungement.

Stigma - Do not be embarrassed by friends or close companions who perform an online background check and discover that you have an arrest on your record. Expunge the stigma!

Laws change - Laws change frequently. If you wait too long to expunge your record, you may find that the law has changed and you are no longer eligible to expunge your criminal record. Expunge your record now!

Traveling - A criminal record may prevent you from traveling to certain countries. There are some countries, such as Canada, that prohibit you from entering the country to visit, work, or study, if you have any criminal charges or convictions on your record. In some cases, you can overcome your conviction(s) if you wait a few years and prove rehabilitation, apply for record suspension, or apply for a temporary resident permit. However, expunging your criminal record is the preferred option. By expunging your criminal record you can avoid the interrogation and scrutiny that comes along with having a criminal record. In addition, if your record reflects poor character, your visa may be cancelled.

EXPUNGEMENT BASICS: 101

Licensing

Professional and/or business license

A criminal record may prevent you from obtaining certain types of business and/or professional licenses. However, in most cases, an expunged record will allow you to acquire such licenses. For example, you are not legally required to report your expunged record when applying for a job as a teacher, insurance agent, or real estate broker. However, you must report your expunged record when applying for a job in law enforcement and the court system.

Firearm License

To legally possess or own a firearm in New Jersey, you must apply for a gun permit. First-time applicants must complete a Mental Health Records Search Application, Form (SP-66) and an Application for Firearms Purchaser Identification Card and/or Handgun Permit, Form (STS-033). If you are applying for a Permit to Carry a Handgun you must complete the State of New Jersey Application For Permit To Carry A Handgun.

Under New Jersey law, an indictable offense conviction or domestic violence conviction will render you ineligible for a gun permit. Offenses involving actual or threatened violence (e.g. domestic violence), manufacturing or cultivating a controlled substance, or serious trespass or stalking may prevent you from legally owning a firearm in New Jersey. However, an expunged criminal record will restore your gun rights. See S54.; [31]

S3.

Am I Eligible for Expungement?

Before you apply for expungement in the State of New Jersey, you must first determine if you are eligible for expungement. Chapter 52 of Title 2C of the New Jersey Code of Criminal Justice specifies the types of offenses that are expungeable and the requirements that you must satisfy to obtain a court's order granting expungement. In New Jersey, a petitioner may expunge certain types of statutorily approved indictable offenses (crimes), convictions of disorderly persons offenses and petty disorderly person offenses, violations of municipal ordinances, and arrests not resulting in convictions. However, multiple convictions may prevent certain offenses from being expungeable.

In New Jersey, there are several statutory and judicial grounds for denying an expungement. Below is a list of several grounds for denying an expungement.

1.   You are **NOT** eligible due to:

    a.   a prior or subsequent conviction;

    - Were you previously or subsequently convicted of a crime?

    b.   type of conviction or seriousness of the crime;

    - Is it drug, theft, or motor-vehicle related? Were you convicted of a crime not subject to expungement under Chapter 52?

    c.   a pending case;

- civil litigation involving the State or a criminal action.

d. a previous expungement;

e. having more than the allowable number of convictions;

f. dismissed charges in a plea bargain;

g. court records indicating that the case is still open;

h. dismissal of charges after a supervisory treatment or similar program, with certain exceptions;

i. a failure to satisfy the waiting period requirement;

j. unpaid fines or court assessments; or

k. charges being dismissed against you because you were found not guilty by reason of insanity.

2. The prosecutor or a government agency objects to your petition and is successful at convincing the court that granting your expungement is not in the best interest of the public.

- The court may deny expungement if the state proves "[t]he need for the availability of records" outweighs the "desirability of having a person freed from any disabilities" arising from the conviction.

3. There was an inaccuracy in the court file.

4. Your application for expungement was not completed or submitted correctly.

S4.

Expungement Eligibility Test

Imagine applying for expungement only to discover that you have wasted valuable time and money on court costs and mailing fees because you are not eligible for expungement. The court will not reimburse you for court costs and mailing fees if it denies your petition for expungement. Therefore, before you apply for expungement, you must determine if your conviction(s) qualify for expungement. A quick and simple eligibility check can save you a lot of time and money.

Chapter 52 of Title 2C of the New Jersey Code of Criminal Justice creates specific eligibility criteria for individuals seeking expungement. The first step in expunging your criminal record is to request your criminal record and determine if you are eligible for expungement. Certain indictable offenses and combinations of offenses are not eligible for expungement in New Jersey. However, your expungement eligibility can quickly and easily be determined by taking we call the smelly New Jersey "FEET." "FEET" stands for Free Expungement Eligibility Test, and of course, we offer "FEET" for our prospective clients at www.legalcleanup.com. Our free eligibility test automatically figures out whether your conviction is eligible for expungement. You simply answer a few basic questions and our automated test will inform you as to which, if any of your offenses, are eligible for expungement. It only takes a few simple clicks to discover if your conviction is eligible for expungement.

S5.

Get A Copy of Your Criminal Record

There are four (4) ways to get a copy of your criminal record:

1.   County Courthouse (Court Disposition)

2.   New Jersey State Police Department (Morpho Trust)

3.   FBI

4.   Your Lawyer

Why do I need a copy of my criminal record?

You will need the case information from your criminal record to complete your application for expungement.

How do I request a copy of my criminal record from the county courthouse?

1.   County Courthouse

You must request a certified disposition from the Criminal Division in the county where charges were filed. Most courts require you to request a record by filling out a Record Request Form. The procedure required to request your criminal record

EXPUNGEMENT BASICS: 101

may vary by court. Therefore, you must contact the appropriate county court to determine the correct process (See Appendix B). A court disposition is a file that indicates the final settlement or outcome of your criminal case. It provides information on the specifics of your arrest or conviction. This includes a judge's ruling, regardless of level of resolution. The court disposition will include all the information you will need to apply for a basic expungement in New Jersey. Your court disposition will reveal the following information:

    a.   Your date of birth.

    b.   Your date of arrest.

    c.   The statutes related to your arrest(s) and/or conviction(s).

    d.   The offense(s) for which you were arrested or charged and of which you were convicted.

    e.   The original indictment, summons or complaint number.

    f.   Your date of conviction, or date of disposition of the matter if no conviction resulted.

    g.   The court's disposition of the matter and the punishment imposed, if any.

There are two options available for you to obtain your criminal record from the county courthouse. You can either mail your criminal record request to the appropriate county court which could take approximately 2-3 weeks for the entire process; or you can personally obtain your criminal record from the county courthouse the same day.

    a.   You must have at least the defendant's name AND the Indictment Number or Case Number or Nature and Date of Offense to process a records request. If you do not have the Indictment, Case Number or Nature and Date of Offense, you may use the New Jersey Courts Public Access Database (Criminal Cases: PROMIS/Gavel Public Case Management System) to look up the case to obtain the proper identifiers. [7]

EXPUNGEMENT BASICS: 101

Fee(s):

The following fees apply:

Copy Fees

$5.00 per document - Certified / $10.00 per document - Exemplified

---

Advantages:

- You will have access to all the information you will need to expunge your criminal record.

- The record request form is easy to complete and the mailing instructions are simple.

- Fast to receive with the option of physically going to the county courthouse to obtain your certified disposition.

- This is the option most lawyers use.

Disadvantages:

- If you have been arrested multiple times in different courts you will have to request your record from each court.

- The procedure to request a record may vary by court. Therefore, you must contact the appropriate county courthouse to determine the process.

How do I request a copy of my criminal record from the New Jersey State Police Department?

2.	NJ State Police Department

To obtain your criminal history record or rap sheet from the New Jersey State Police Department you must schedule an appointment to have your fingerprints recorded by Morpho Trust. You must contact Morpho Trust to schedule a time and place to have your fingerprints taken. The quickest and easiest way to schedule your   appointment is via the Web at www.identogo.com/FP/NewJersey.aspx or www.bioapplicant.com/nj. [20]

Advantages:

- The background check will scan throughout the 21 counties in New Jersey for all of your arrests.

- There is a comparably short waiting period.

Disadvantages:

- Forms instructions are long and cumbersome.

- You must travel to a MorphoTrust USA fingerprinting location.

- If you work or have a busy schedule, business hours may be inconvenient.

- If you were not fingerprinted during processing, the arrest may not be present in your criminal history record.

- May or may not include juvenile or family records.

How do I request a copy of my criminal record from the Federal Bureau of Investigation (FBI)?

3.   FBI Search

To obtain your criminal history record from the FBI you must fill out an application and the appropriate fingerprint card. Unlike obtaining your record from the New Jersey State Police, the FBI does not require you to travel to a fingerprinting location. However, the FBI does recommend having your fingerprints taken by a fingerprint technician. According to the FBI website, processing may take approximately five (5) to six (6) weeks depending on the volume of request received. [21]

EXPUNGEMENT BASICS: 101

Fee:

$18

Advantages:

- All arrests throughout each state in the country where you were fingerprinted will be present.

- You are not required to travel to a fingerprinting location. However, we strongly recommend that you do.

Disadvantages:

- Forms instructions are long and cumbersome.

- Completing your fingerprint on your own may be difficult.

- Could take a minimum of five (5) to six (6) weeks to receive your record.

- If you were not fingerprinted during processing, the arrest may not be present in your criminal history record / summary.

- May or may not include juvenile or family records.

How do I request a copy of my criminal record from my attorney?

4.	Your Attorney

You can request a copy of your court disposition from the attorney that handled your case, by requesting your criminal record from him or her.

S6.

Expungement Forms

To apply for expungement in New Jersey, there are several documents you must prepare. The New Jersey Judiciary offers self-represented litigants an expungement packet which includes all the forms you will need to expunge a criminal record with less than four (4) arrest(s) and/or conviction(s). The forms are downloadable from the New Jersey Courts On-Line Self-Help Center at http://www.judiciary.sta te.nj.us/prose/index.htm#criminal. See Appendix J for sample forms only; [8]

If you want to represent yourself and you have no more than three (3) arrests and/or convictions, you may use the New Jersey Judiciary expungement packet. At www.legalcleanup.com, our automated system will assemble and generate the basic expungement forms for you for a small fee. You simply answer a few basic questions and our automated system will assemble and generate the completed documents for you.

However, if you have more than three (3) arrests and/or convictions, or if your case is complex, you cannot use the downloadable forms at the New Jersey Help Center without some modification or redrafting. In this case, you must either modify the New Jersey Judiciary expungement packet or create your own set of expungement documents. At www.legalcleanup.com, we will assemble and generate the expungement forms for you for a small fee. You simply answer a few basic questions and we will assemble and generate the completed documents for you.

Using the New Jersey Judiciary Expungement Packet there are a total of seven (7) forms you must complete and submit to the appropriate court(s) and government agencies. You must complete the forms with 100% accuracy. Be sure to follow all guidelines and procedures when filling out such forms to prevent your expungement application from being rejected. The process of filing and mailing your expungement paperwork is a time-consuming and arduous task. That is why Vonnie C. Dones III, ESQ. at www.legalcleanup.com is here to help you throughout the entire process.

The seven (7) forms you must complete to expunge your criminal record using the New Jersey Judiciary Expungement Packet are as follows:

Reminder - Request for a State Police Record

You must enclose your fingerprint card from Morpho Trust (Safran). There is a $30 fee (money order or certified check) payable to the Division of State Police. However, you do not have to make a State Police Record Request if you decide to obtain your record from your lawyer, the FBI, or the county court where your arrest and/or conviction occurred. See S5.

1. **Form A** - Petition for Expungement

A Petition for Expungement is a document asking the court to expunge "the complaints, warrants, arrests, commitments, processing records, fingerprints, photographs, index cards, rap sheets, and judicial docket records" on your record. N.J.C.A. 2C:52-1. This includes electronic records as well. You must list your entire criminal history, including any out-of-state convictions and/or arrests. In addition, you must list your name, the date of your arrest, municipality, name of the offense, statute, original indictment / accusation / summons / docket number / warrant number / complaint number, date of sentence, and sentence. Sign and print your name at the bottom of the form. You must then print your name and sign the Verification page in the presence of a notary public. The notary public will then sign the Verification page at the bottom and affix their seal to the page. To complete Form A you will need a copy of your criminal record as previously stated.

2. **Form B** - Order for Hearing

An Order of Expungement is a court document setting a hearing date and time. It is rare that a petitioner would have to make an appearance or attend a hearing. You must fill out your personal information and list the agencies that you will send copies of the Order and Petition. Be sure to send copies to all required agencies via certified mail, return receipt within five (5) days of the Order.

3. Form C - Expungement Order

The Expungement Order is a document signed by a Judge from the Superior Court of New Jersey ordering that your listed conviction(s) and/or arrest(s) be expunged. You must mail the expungement order via certified mail, return receipt to the required government agencies listed in the Order. Once the agencies receive the Order, each agency must comply with the court's order and remove your expunged arrest(s) and/or conviction(s) from their database and /or records. You must complete this form by filling out your personal information.

4. Form D - Cover Letter

You will use this letter as a cover sheet when mailing (certified mail, return receipt) the PETITION, ORDER FOR HEARING, and PROPOSED FINAL ORDER to the county court where your arrest and prosecution occurred. This letter informs the county court that you are applying for expungement. Attach the cover letter to the front of all three (3) copies of the PETITION, ORDER FOR HEARING, and PROPOSED FINAL ORDER. You must also fill out your personal information, government agency information, and provide your signature at the bottom of this cover letter.

5. Form E - Cover Letter

You will use this letter as a cover sheet when mailing (certified mail, return receipt) the PETITION, ORDER FOR HEARING, and PROPOSED FINAL ORDER to the various government agencies in New Jersey giving each department notice of hearing. Attach the cover letter to the front of all copies of your forms sent to the various government agencies. Complete this form by filling out your personal information, government agency information, and providing your signature at the bottom of the form.

EXPUNGEMENT BASICS: 101

6.   **Form F** - Proof of Notice

Proof of Notice is a document indicating that you, as the petitioner, have satisfied your obligation of mailing and notifying all applicable government agencies of your application for expungement. It will include your scheduled hearing date and time. You must provide Proof of Notice, if required by the county court from which you are seeking relief. You must provide your signature at the bottom of the form indicating that you have enclosed the green return receipt cards (certified mail receipts) that you used to mail the PETITION, ORDER FOR HEARING, and PROPOSED FINAL ORDER to the applicable government agencies. You MUST contact the appropriate New Jersey Criminal Case Management Office to determine whether Proof of Notice (Form G) is necessary in your case.

7.   **Form G** - Cover Letter

Use this letter as a cover sheet when mailing the EXPUNGEMENT ORDER signed by the judge to the appropriate government agencies. Complete this form by filling out your personal information, the appropriate agency information, and providing your signature at the bottom of the form. You must also fill out the Certified Mail Number at the bottom of the form.

S7.

10 Steps to Expungement

NOTE BEFORE YOU CONTINUE:

If you decide to purchase our expungement services at www.legalcleanup.com you must first register to open a client account. You can then log into your account to begin filling out your expungement paperwork. You will then be asked to complete a simple questionnaire. After you complete the questionnaire, our automated system will assemble and generate the completed expungement forms for you. For a few extra bucks, the Law Firm of Vonnie C. Dones III, ESQ. can review your automated documents for accuracy. Or, we can complete all of your expungement paperwork and mail it to the appropriate court(s) and government agencies for you. You do not have to fill-out, mail or file any forms, unless you prefer to do so. However, if you choose to "Do-It-Yourself," you must complete the following 10 steps. **Reminder:** Make sure you are eligible for an expungement by taking our Free (Expungement) Eligibility Test at www.legalcleanup.com.

The following steps to expungement are outlined in the expungement packet provided by the New Jersey Courts On-Line Self-Help Center at http://www.judiciary.state.nj.us/prose/index.htm#criminal and have been summarized as follows: (See Appendix J for sample forms only); [8]

EXPUNGEMENT BASICS: 101

Step 1.

Request a copy of your criminal record, "rap sheet," or certified disposition (Form A) from:

- County Courthouse (Superior Court Criminal Case Management Office in the county where your arrest or conviction occurred)

- NJ State Police Department (Criminal Information Unit) MorphoTrust USA / Safran Group

- FBI

- Your Lawyer

Step 2.

Fill out the following appropriate forms using a copy of your criminal record.

- Petition for Expungement - (Form A)

- Order for Hearing - (Form B)

- Expungement Order - (Form C)

- Cover Letter - (Form D)

Step 3.

Sign the Verification page at the end of the Petition for Expungement (Form A) in the presence of a notary public.

- Make three (3) copies of your notarized Petition for Expungement (Form A), Order of Hearing (Form B), and proposed Expungement Order (Form C). Be sure to keep one (1) copy of Form A, B, and C for your personal record. You will mail the other two copies to the appropriate county courthouse as indicated in Step 5.

Step 4.

Attach the Cover Letter (Form D) to each of the three (3) copies of Forms A through C.

Step 5.

File and serve two copies of Forms A through D to the New Jersey Criminal Case Management Office in the county courthouse where your arrest and/or prosecution occurred.

- Include two large self-addressed envelopes with the appropriate postage stamped on each envelope.

Step 6.

A few weeks later, you will receive a FILED copy of your forms with an assigned DOCKET NUMBER. The Order of Hearing will also state the date and time of your hearing.

- Immediately make at least seven (7) copies of the Petition for Expungement, Order for Hearing, and the proposed Expungement Order.

Note: It is very rare that a petitioner will have to make an appearance or attend a hearing.

Step 7.

Mail one (1) copy of Forms A through C to EACH of the first seven (7) government agencies listed below via certified mail, return receipt requested. Each copy MUST have a separate Cover Letter (Form E). You must fill in the "Certified Mail No." at the bottom of (Form E). Only mail a copy of Forms A through C to each of the last four (4) government agencies listed below if applicable to your case.

- The Attorney General of New Jersey.

- The Superintendent of State Police, Expungement Unit.

- The County Prosecutor.

- The Magistrate or the Court Clerk of the municipal court if a municipal court heard the matter.

- The Chief of Police or other head of the police department where the offense was committed or the arrest was made.

- The chief law enforcement officer of any other law enforcement agency of this state that participated in the arrest.

- The Warden or Superintendant (Administrator) of any institution in which you were incarcerated.

- For State Grand Jury Cases Only: Division of Criminal Justice Attention: Records and Identification 25 Market Street P.O. Box 085 Trenton, NJ 08625

- The County Probation Division must be provided a copy of Forms A through C if you were granted a conditional discharge, conditional dismissal, enrolled into a Pretrial Intervention (PTI) Program or a juvenile diversion program (juvenile conference committee or intake service conference), granted a deferred disposition, performed community service, owed fines or restitution or you served a term of probation.

- The Division of Criminal Justice, Records and Identification Unit should be provided a copy if your case was processed through the State Grand Jury.

- The County Family Division should be provided a copy if you are requesting the expungement of any juvenile delinquency matters.

Note: You SHOULD mail the copies of these forms right away, as the statute mandates service or mailing WITHIN FIVE (5) DAYS from the date of the order. (N.J.S.A. 2C:52-10)

Step 8.

Contact the New Jersey Criminal Case Management Office to determine whether Proof of Notice (Form F) is necessary.

- Proof of Notice is a document used to show proof to the court that the Petition for Expungement, Order of Hearing, and Expungement Order was served on and/or mailed to the appropriate government agencies. Thus, Proof of Notice is filed with the court after notice to the appropriate government agencies is given. Proof of Notice must include the green return receipt cards.

Step 9.

Attend Hearing (if necessary / rare, unless a prosecutor or government agency objects)

Step 10.

Mail Expungement Order with the judge's signature to the appropriate government agencies via certified mail, return receipt requested. Use Cover Letter (Form G) when mailing the Expungement Order to the applicable government agencies listed below. Each copy must have a separate Cover Letter (Form G). You must fill in the "Certified Mail No." at the bottom of (Form G). Immediately after you receive a copy of the Expungement Order signed by the judge and stamped "Filed" by the court, mail one copy of the Expungement Order, by certified mail, return receipt requested, to each of the following applicable government agencies:

EXPUNGEMENT BASICS: 101

- The Attorney General of New Jersey.

- The Superintendent of State Police, Expungement Unit.

- The County Prosecutor.

- The Magistrate or the Court Clerk of the municipal court if a municipal court heard the matter.

- The Chief of Police or other head of the police department where the offense was committed or the arrest was made.

- The chief law enforcement officer of any other law enforcement agency of this state that participated in the arrest.

- The Warden or Superintendant (Administrator) of any institution in which you were incarcerated.

- For State Grand Jury Cases Only: Division of Criminal Justice Attention: Records and Identification 25 Market Street P.O. Box 085 Trenton, NJ 08625

- The County Probation Division should be served or provided a copy if you were granted a conditional discharge, conditional dismissal, enrolled into a Pretrial Intervention (PTI) Program, or enrolled in a juvenile diversion program (juvenile conference committee or intake service conference), granted a deferred disposition, performed community service, owed fines or restitution or you served a term of probation.

- The Division of Criminal Justice, Records and Identification Unit should be provided a copy if your case was processed through the State Grand Jury.

- The County Family Division should be provided a copy if you are requesting the expungement of any juvenile delinquency matters.

S8.

Court Costs and Mailing Fees

Applicants are responsible for paying all court costs and mailing fees when applying for an expungement in New Jersey. The new 2014 cost of sending a 1-ounce USPS Certified Mail letter with Return Receipt (green card) is $6.48. You will need to pay for photocopying, envelopes, and stamps. There is a filing fee of $52.50. Most offices do not accept personal checks, so you should include a money order or certified check made out to the State of N.J. Treasurer. The approximate costs of applying for an expungement are as follows:

1.	Court filing fee:	$52.50
2.	Certified Mail w/ Return Receipt:	$110.16 - $123.12
3.	Photocopying:	$20
4.	Envelopes / Stamps:	$15 - $35 (regular mail, not including priority, or express mail)
	Average (approximate) total cost:	$214.14
*	The average total cost does not include the cost to obtain a copy of your criminal history record. The price for a copy of your criminal record will vary depending on the option you choose to obtain your criminal record. See S5.	

EXPUNGEMENT BASICS: 101

This amount varies depending on a applicant's shipping choice. If you make a mistake in filing your petition you may have to re-apply for expungement and bear all costs associated with re-applying. The State may issue a refund for the court costs, but not for the mailing fees. If you decide to use the FedEx Office Print Online service, you can print your documents from your home computer, tablet, or phone and your order will be available for pick-up at a nearby FedEx location. However, choosing an on-line option will result in an increase in photocopying costs. Currently, the charge to use the FedEx Office Print Online service is 0.22¢ per page. FedEx Office Print Online offers 128-bit SSL encryption, customer log-in protection, and VeriSign Extended Validation (EV) Certificates. Visit the FedEx Customer Protection Center at http://www.fedex.com/us/security/our-part/index.html for updates and/or possible risks in printing your documents using FedEx Office Print Online.

S9.

Expungement Process

Once you have filed your petition, it may take a minimum of 3-4 months to obtain an Order of Expungement. Generally, the following timeline would occur when expunging your criminal record in New Jersey.

1. Week (1-6) - File and serve your Petition for Expungement and accompanying documents to the appropriate county courthouse and wait to receive it back from the county courthouse.

2. Week (6-7) - Mail the FILED copy of your Petition to each of the applicable government agencies via certified mail, return receipt requested.

3. Week (7-12) - Contact the New Jersey Criminal Case Management Office in the appropriate county courthouse to determine whether Proof of Notice (Form G) is necessary. The county courthouse will update its records. You must then mail the Order of Expungement to the appropriate government agencies for compliance. The agencies will then update their records and this normally takes 30-60 days.

S10.

Prosecutor or Government Agency Objects to Your Petition

A prosecutor or government agency may object to your petition for the following reasons:

1. **Sale or distribution of drugs or possession with the intent to sell drugs**

    A recent amendment to New Jersey expungement law permits a petitioner to expunge certain types of drug distribution offenses. See S11. However, because New Jersey law governing expungement of drug distribution convictions has recently changed, a prosecutor is likely to object. An in-court hearing will be required if a prosecutor or government agency objects.

2. **"Early Pathway" expungement**

    You are applying for an "early pathway" expungement. A recent statutory amendment to New Jersey expungement law provides a petitioner with an early pathway to expunging statutorily approved indictable offenses or crimes. Rather than having to wait ten (10) years to expunge your criminal conviction, the amendment allows a petitioner to expunge his or her criminal conviction after five (5) years. See S.22. A prosecutor is likely to object to such a case. An in-court hearing will be required if a prosecutor or government agency objects.

3.   **Crime Spree doctrine**

You have committed multiple crimes during a single event or quickly after each other. New Jersey judicial law will determine if you are eligible for expungement under the New Jersey crime spree doctrine. A prosecutor is likely to object to such a case. An in-court hearing will be required if a prosecutor or government agency objects.

4.   **Public Interest case**

The prosecutor finds that (1) expungement will not be in the best interest of the public (the court finds the need for preservation of your records outweigh the benefits of expungement), (2) the crime was too dangerous to be expunged, or (3) the petitioner's behavior after the crime does not prove rehabilitation.

5.   **Conviction(s) are not eligible for expungement**

The prosecutor finds that you do not qualify for expungement.

6.   **Incorrectly completed expungement application**

Your application contains a mistake and/or was filed incorrectly.

S11.

Expunging Your Criminal Record More Than Once

The general rule is that you can only expunge your criminal record one time. It is important that you properly prepare your petition for expungement the first time. Make sure you list all of your arrests and/or convictions by obtaining a complete criminal history summary. If you have received an expungement for a criminal conviction once and are subsequently convicted of another offense, you cannot expunge the latter offense, unless you qualify under the following two exceptions. N.J.S.A. 2C:52-14

Two Exceptions:

1. You can expunge subsequent criminal arrests and/or charges that are dismissed and/or do not result in convictions. An arrest may not lead to a conviction if there is a finding of not guilty, insufficient evidence, a dismissal by prosecution for unknown reasons, or participation in a diversion program.

2. If you have previously expunged a criminal conviction and are seeking to expunge of a subsequent municipal ordinance violation, the subsequent municipal ordinance violation is expungeable.

EXPUNGEMENT BASICS: 101

NOTE: You are not eligible for expungement under the "diversion program" if you have a prior conviction for a controlled substance offense.

S12.

Expungement Hearing

After filing your petition with the court, the judge will schedule a hearing by signing the Order for Hearing form provided by you in your petition. In most instances, you do not have to attend a hearing or make an appearance unless the prosecutor or a government agency objects to your petition for expungement.

After being served with your petition, the prosecutor or a government agency may elect to object to your petition any time before or at the hearing. If the prosecutor or a government agency objects to your petition before the hearing, their office will send you a letter informing you of their reasons for objecting to your petition. On the day of your hearing, you should be prepared to respond to any objections the prosecutor or a government agency may have in regard to your petition. An objection by a prosecutor or government agency does not mean your expungement is denied. It simply means that you must prove to the court that your arrest(s) and/or conviction(s) should be expunged.

After hearing arguments on both sides, the judge will make a decision to either grant or deny your expungement. The judge will then notify you by letter of the court's decision. If your expungement is granted, it typically takes 30-60 days to remove it from public record.

EXPUNGEMENT BASICS: 101

How To Prepare For A Court Hearing

1. Attend and Be On Time

You must comply with a judge's order to attend a court hearing or run the risk of your expungement being denied by default. If you cannot attend your court hearing on the scheduled date and time, you must call the Judge's clerk and notify the court of your situation. Depending on the circumstances of your case, the court will likely reschedule your court hearing.

If you are scheduled to attend a court hearing, be prompt and on time. Being late to your court hearing can also result in your petition being denied by default. You should plan on arriving at the courthouse at least 30 minutes before your scheduled hearing.

2. Bring Your Paperwork

Be sure to bring your original expungement paperwork and two (2) copies of your expungement paperwork to court. In addition, you should bring a pen and pad to take notes during your hearing. You must bring your entire file with you to court, in the event the judge requests any of your paperwork or has any questions in regard to your petition for expungement.

3. Bring A Short Draft Of Your Argument

Be sure to lay out and organize any argument or information you may have in support of your petition for expungement. Prepare a coherent and convincing argument disproving the prosecutor's or a government agency's objection to your petition for expungement. Create a list of checkpoints to ensure that you cover all relevant topics in a logical and organized manner.

4. Bring Evidence To Support Your Argument

Be prepared to present evidence and/or witnesses to prove your case in court. If you become unsure as to what evidence you must present to the court, you should contact the Judge's clerk for more information. Again, be sure to bring your original expungement paperwork and two (2) copies of your expungement paperwork to court. In addition, become familiar with state and local rules of civil procedure and New Jersey Rules of Evidence.

5. Dress Professional

Be sure to adhere to local rules on dress code. A good rule of thumb is to always dress professional when appearing in court. Men should wear a traditional black suit with a solid color tie; and women should wear a skirt suit with heels and hosiery. You should also be properly groomed.

6. Courtroom Etiquette

You must adhere to the local rules of decorum and procedure. When you first address the court you should say, "May it please the court, my name is..." When addressing the judge, start by saying "Your Honor." You must ask permission to approach a witness and be respectful to court staff and opposing counsel. Cell phones and certain types of electronic devices are not permitted in court. A good rule of thumb is to always remain professional, respectful, and polite when appearing in court.

7. Politely Ask Questions

If you have difficulty understanding what is happening in court or become confused about what happens next, politely ask the judge to explain the situation. Because you are a pro se litigant, the judge will likely show leniency and help you navigate through the process.

S13.

Notice of Hearing

You, as the petitioner, must provide Notice of an Expungement Hearing to any government agency with relevant records. First, you must mail the Order for Hearing to the appropriate county courthouse and wait a few weeks to receive it back from the county courthouse. You must then mail the signed Order for Hearing to the appropriate agencies within five (5) days from the date the judge signed the order.

S14.

DMV Records

Motor-related offenses are not expungeable in New Jersey which includes any offense under Title 39 of the New Jersey Code, namely vehicle and traffic regulation offenses. In addition, DUI (Driving Under the Influence) offenses are not eligible for expungement under Title 39 of the New Jersey Code. [2]

CHAPTER 2:
WAITING PERIODS

S15.

Waiting Period Requirement for Specific Types of Offenses

Before you can expunge your criminal conviction, you must wait until the statutory waiting period has expired. New Jersey law requires that a petitioner who wishes to expunge his or her conviction wait a specific period of time before he or she can expunge the conviction. There are different waiting periods which depends on the type and level of the offense. The higher the level of the offense, the longer the waiting period. The following is a summary of the waiting time requirements for specific types of offenses in New Jersey. [1]

WAITING PERIODS

Waiting Period Requirements

Nature of Offense	Waiting Time
Indictable Offense / Crime	Ten (10) years. However, the court will consider an application to expunge a crime after five (5) years. (The court refers to this as "early pathway.") For early pathway, the court will require you to show that granting the expungement is in the public interest.
Disorderly Persons Offense	Five (5) years
Petty Disorderly Persons Offense	Five (5) years
Juvenile Adjudication	Five (5) years, or period for equivalent offense if committed by an adult, whichever is less.
Municipal Ordinance	Two (2) years
Young Drug Offender (21 years of age or younger when offense was committed)	One (1) year
Completion of Diversion Program (PTI, Conditional Discharge, or Conditional Dismissal)	Six (6) months
Not guilty by reason of insanity, or not guilty for lack of mental capacity	These dispositions cannot be expunged.
Final Restraining Order arising from domestic violence situation	Records relating to restraining orders cannot be expunged because restraining orders are civil in nature, not criminal.
Dismissal, Acquittal, Discharge Without a Conviction or Finding of Guilt. (Arrest)	No waiting time at all.

S16.

When Does The Waiting Period Start?

After you determine how long you must wait to expunge your conviction, you must then precisely identify your waiting period start time. You must calculate the waiting period for the offense using an accurate starting time to ensure expungement eligibility. If you miscalculate the start time, you run the risk of your expungement being denied. If the judge denies your expungement, he or she may elect to further deny you the opportunity to re-apply for expungement. Below is a summary of the waiting period start times for the following offenses. [1]; [3]

1.   **Indictable Offense** (Crime)

   •   **Ten (10) years from**
            date of conviction, payment of fines, satisfactory completion of
            probation or parole, or release from incarceration,
            WHICHEVER IS LATER.

Note: Under the amended New Jersey Statute, the 10-year waiting period required to expunge an indictable offense is reduced to 5 years, if the court finds that expungement is in the best interest of the public and the petitioner meets all other statutory requirements. In addition, if 10 years has passed since the indictable conviction and the petitioner failed to pay his fines, he is still eligible for expungement if 1) the Court finds that the petitioner substantially complied with a court ordered payment plan pursuant to N.J.S.2C:46-1 et seq; or (2) the petitioner could not pay his or her fines because of "compelling circumstances."

WAITING PERIODS

2. **Disorderly Persons Offense and Petty Disorderly Persons Offense**

   - **Five (5) years from**
       date of conviction, payment of fines, satisfactory completion of probation or parole, or release from incarceration, WHICHEVER IS LATER.

3. **Municipal Ordinance Violation**

   - **Two (2) years from**
       date of conviction, payment of fines, satisfactory completion of probation or parole, or release from incarceration, WHICHEVER IS LATER.

4. **Young Drug Offenders**

   - **One (1) year from**
       date of conviction, termination of probation or parole or discharge from custody, WHICHEVER IS LATER.

5. **Diversion/Supervisory Treatment Program** - (Pre-Trial Intervention (PTI), Conditional Discharge, or Conditional Dismissal)

   - **Six-months from**
       the entry of the order of dismissal.

6. **Dismissal, Acquittal, Discharge Without A Conviction or Finding of Guilt**. (Arrest)

   - From the entry of the order of dismissal.

CHAPTER 3:
CLASSIFICATION OF OFFENSES

S17.

Types of Offenses

An offense is a wrongdoing committed against society. If a person commits a wrongdoing prohibited by law, he or she has committed an offense. Offenses are punishable by law. Under the 10th Amendment of the United States Constitution, each state has the power to make its own laws. Federalism divides power between the federal and state governments. Federal laws preempt conflicting state laws, however, the federal government has limited powers "to make laws." Often, the federal, state, and local governments share powers. Therefore, the New Jersey Code of Criminal Justice, municipal ordinances, and state common law governs the type of offenses legally prohibited in New Jersey, unless such laws are preempted by federal law.

There are four (4) general categories of offenses in New Jersey:

1.   Indictable Offenses (Crimes)

2.   Disorderly Persons Offenses or Petty Disorderly Persons Offenses

3.   Municipal Ordinance Violations

4.   Motor Vehicle or Traffic Offenses

An indictable offense is a "criminal" offense. All other categories of offenses, including motor vehicle or traffic offenses, disorderly persons or petty disorderly persons offenses, and municipal ordinance violations in New Jersey are not

CLASSIFICATION OF OFFENSES

considered "criminal" offenses. Such offenses are lesser offenses. All indictable offenses or crimes are heard in the superior court in the county in which the alleged crime occurred. All cases involving lesser offenses are heard in the municipal courts of limited jurisdiction. New Jersey has three trial courts, namely the superior court, the tax court, and the municipal court. In addition, New Jersey has two appellate courts, namely the supreme court and the appellate division of the superior court.

S18.

Indictable Offenses

What is known as a "felony" in many other states is an indictable offense in New Jersey. New Jersey has abolished the felony classification and the term "felony" is no longer used. In New Jersey, a crime is an indictable offense, not a "felony." However, in State v. Doyle, the New Jersey courts recognized that indictable offenses or crimes in New Jersey are "equatable" to felonies. 200 A.2d 606 (N.J. 1964) All persons accused of indictable offenses or crimes are entitled to an indictment by a grand jury or a trial by jury. Indictable offenses are classified into 1st, 2nd, 3rd, and 4th degrees. N.J.S.A. 2C:43-1; [4] The most serious offenses are in the first degree category. "Indictable" means that a grand jury has found that there is enough evidence to support a formal charge and require that the defendant stand trial for the crime. In New Jersey, crimes are offenses that carry sentences of six (6) months of jail or more. If an offender is sentenced to one year or more, he or she will serve time in state prison, unless there is a county penitentiary or workhouse. N.J.S.A.2C:43-10(a) and (b).

- First degree crimes include, but are not limited to, murder, manslaughter, drug distribution (large quantities) aggravated sexual assault, and rape. A first degree crime carries a 10-20 year mandatory prison sentence or between 20, 25 or 30 years and life for certain crimes, such as murder and a fine up to $200,000. N.J.S.A. 2C:11-3; N.J.S.A. 2C:43-10; [4] For first degree crimes there is a presumption of incarceration which means that it is presumed that the judge will sentence an offender to state prison. A competent attorney can help you overcome a presumption of incarceration.

- Second degree crimes include, but are not limited to, certain sex crimes, aggravated arson, burglary, robbery with a weapon, kidnapping, white collar crimes, and drug crimes (small quantities). A second degree crime carries a 5-10 year mandatory prison sentence and a fine up to $150,000. [4] For second degree crimes there is a presumption of incarceration which means that it is presumed that the judge will sentence an offender to state prison. A competent attorney can help you overcome a presumption of incarceration.

- Third degree crimes can include, but are not limited to, arson, some robbery offenses, some driving under the influence (DUI) offenses, possession of cocaine, ecstasy, or heroin (controlled substances), possession of a handgun, certain thefts, and aggravated assault. A third degree crime carries a 3-5 year mandatory prison sentence and can be fined up to $15,000. [4] For third degree crimes there is a presumption of non-incarceration. Therefore, the judge, at his or her discretion, may sentence the defendant to probation in lieu of a prison term. He may sentence the defendant to serve all or part of his sentence on probation in lieu of state prison.

- Fourth degree crimes include, but are not limited to, stalking, unauthorized use of a motor vehicle, some charges involving assault and threat crimes, possession of marijuana, criminal sexual contact, stalking, some robbery offenses, some DUI offenses, and forgery. A fourth degree crime is punishable by up to 18 months in prison and a fine of up to $10,000. [4] For fourth degree crimes there is a presumption of non-incarceration. Therefore, the judge, at his or her discretion, may sentence the defendant to probation in lieu of a prison term. He may sentence the defendant to serve all or part of his sentence on probation in lieu of state prison.

S19.

Requirements for Indictable Offense Expungement

Under New Jersey law, a petitioner must satisfy certain statutory requirements to expunge an indictable offense (crime). Below is an outline of the statutory requirements for expunging an indictable offense. [1]; [4]

- **Statute:** N.J.S.A. 2C:52-2

- **Waiting Period:** Ten (10) years from date of conviction, payment of fines, satisfactory completion of probation or parole, or release from incarceration, whichever is later.

- **Other Convictions:** No other prior or subsequent indictable offenses (crimes) in New Jersey or elsewhere, no more than two other disorderly persons or petty disorderly persons offenses.

- **Note:** Under the amended New Jersey Statute, the 10-year waiting period required to expunge an indictable offense is reduced to five (5) years, if the court finds that expungement is in the best interest of the public and the petitioner meets all other statutory requirements. Under this "early pathway" scenario, the petitioner has the burden of proving to the court that expungement is in the best interest of the public. Therefore, under N.J.S.A. 2C:52:2(2), a person seeking an "early pathway" expungement must wait until "at least five years has expired from the date of his conviction, payment of fine, satisfactory completion of probation or parole, or release from

77

CLASSIFICATION OF OFFENSES

incarceration, whichever is later...[.]" Certain criminal convictions are not eligible for expungement.

- **Non-Expungeable Indictable Offenses or Crimes:**

1. The following indictable offenses or crimes can never be expunged. [1]; [4]

    - Crimes of murder, manslaughter, treason, anarchy, kidnapping, rape, forcible sodomy, arson, perjury, false swearing, robbery, embracery, or a conspiracy or any attempt to commit any of the foregoing, or aiding, assisting or concealing persons accused of the foregoing crimes, shall not be expunged.

    - Records of conviction for the following crimes specified in the New Jersey Code of Criminal Justice shall not be subject to expungement: Section 2C:11-1 et seq. (Criminal Homicide), except death by auto as specified in section 2C:11-5; section 2C:13-1 (Kidnapping); section 2C:13-6 (Luring or Enticing); section 1 of P.L.2005, c. 77 (C.2C:13-8) (Human Trafficking); section 2C:14-2 (Aggravated Sexual Assault); section 2C:14-3a (Aggravated Criminal Sexual Contact); if the victim is a minor, section 2C:14-3b (Criminal Sexual Contact); if the victim is a minor and the offender is not the parent of the victim, section 2C:13-2 (Criminal Restraint) or section 2C:13-3 (False Imprisonment); section 2C:15-1 (Robbery); section 2C:17-1 (Arson and Related Offenses); section 2C:24-4a. (Endangering the welfare of a child by engaging in sexual conduct which would impair or debauch the morals of the child); section 2C:24-4b(4) (Endangering the welfare of a child); section 2C:24-4b. (3) (Causing or permitting a child to engage in a prohibited sexual act); section 2C:24:4b.(5)(a) (Selling or manufacturing child pornography); section 2C:28-1 (Perjury); section 2C:28-2 (False Swearing); section 2C:34-1b. (4) (Knowingly promoting the prostitution of the actor's child); section 2 of P.L.2002, c.26 (C.2C:38-2) (Terrorism); subsection a. of section 3 of P.L.2002, c. 26 (C.2C:38-3) (Producing or Possessing Chemical Weapons, Biological Agents or Nuclear or Radiological Devices); and conspiracies or attempts to commit such crimes.

    - Records of conviction for any crime committed by a person holding any public office, position or employment, elective or appointive, under the government of this State or any agency or political subdivision thereof and any conspiracy or attempt to commit such a crime shall not be subject to expungement if the crime involved or touched such office, position or employment.

2. Sale or distribution of a controlled dangerous substance (CDS) or possession thereof with INTENT TO SELL, with some exceptions as listed below.

- Expungement shall be denied EXCEPT where the crimes relate to:

  (1) Marijuana, where the total quantity sold, distributed or possessed with intent to sell was 25 grams or less, or

  (2) Hashish, where the total quantity sold, distributed or possessed with intent to sell was five grams or less.

  (3) Any controlled dangerous substance (CDS) provided that the conviction is of the THIRD or FOURTH degree, where the court finds that expungement is consistent with the PUBLIC INTEREST, giving due consideration to the nature of the offense and the petitioner's character and conduct since conviction. In such cases, the court must consider whether the need for the availability of the records outweighs the petitioner's interest in expunging the records. A hearing is required if any government office objects.

  (4) Convictions for conspiracy to possess, distribute, or sell CDS.

3. Sale, distribution, or possession of a CDS with INTENT TO SELL in the FIRST and SECOND degree is not expungeable.

S20.

Disorderly Persons & Petty Disorderly Persons Offenses

What is known as a "misdemeanor" in many other states is a disorderly persons offense or petty disorderly persons offense in New Jersey. A disorderly persons offense or petty disorderly persons offense is often referred to as a misdemeanor. New Jersey has abolished the misdemeanor classification and the term "misdemeanor" is no longer used. However, the legislature in drafting the New Jersey's Code of Criminal Justice, strangely enough, uses the term "misdemeanor" to mean a "crime of the fourth degree." See e.g., N.J.S.A. 2C:43-1; [4] In New Jersey, a disorderly persons offense carries a maximum penalty of six (6) months in jail and a $1000 fine. A petty disorderly persons offense carries a maximum of thirty days in jail and a $500 fine. The most frequent types of disorderly persons offenses are:

- Underage Possession of Alcohol

- Simple Assault

- Possession of a Fake ID

- Possession of Less than 50 Grams of Marijuana

- Possession of Drug Paraphernalia

- Harassment

CLASSIFICATION OF OFFENSES

- Shoplifting (in an amount less than $200)

- Disorderly Conduct

- Resisting Arrest

- Bad Checks

- Lewdness

S21.

Requirements for Disorderly Persons & Petty Disorderly Persons Offense Expungement

Under New Jersey law, a petitioner must satisfy certain statutory requirements to expunge a disorderly persons or petty disorderly persons offense. Below is an outline of the statutory requirements for expunging such offenses:

- **Statute:** N.J.S.A. 2C:52-3

- **Waiting Period:** Five (5) years from date of conviction, payment of fines, satisfactory completion of probation or parole, or release from incarceration.

- **Other Convictions:** No indictable offenses (crimes) in New Jersey or elsewhere and no more than three (3) other disorderly persons or petty disorderly persons offenses in any state.

S22.

Municipal Ordinance Violation

What is a municipal ordinance?

A municipal ordinance is a law passed by local government, such as city, town, village, township, or borough, as opposed to the State. Ordinances are local laws created to maintain public safety, health, morals, and general welfare. Ordinances may deal with prohibited prescribed levels of noise, public streets and sidewalks, parking, snow removal, littering, public urination, zoning, and restrictions on pets.

What are some types of municipal ordinance violations?

Municipal ordinance violations include drinking in public, having an open container, underage drinking, building code violations, shoplifting, disobedience to lawful orders, harassment, domestic violence, and disturbing the peace. New Jersey currently has 565 municipalities, due to the Princeton Township and Princeton Borough merger on January 1, 2013. All 565 municipalities belong to one of the five types of municipal governments. The maximum fine for a municipal ordinance violation is $2,000; and although rare, such a violation carries a maximum sentence of 90 days in jail or 90 days of community service.

What do I have to do to expunge a municipal ordinance violation?

Under New Jersey law, a petitioner must satisfy certain statutory requirements to expunge a municipal ordinance violation. Below is an outline of the statutory requirements for expunging a municipal ordinance violation.

CLASSIFICATION OF OFFENSES

- **Statute:** N.J.S.A. 2C:52-4

- **Waiting Period:** Two (2) years from date of conviction, payment of fines, satisfactory completion of probation or parole, or release from incarceration.

- **Other Convictions:** No indictable offenses (crimes) in New Jersey or elsewhere. No more than two other disorderly persons or petty disorderly persons offenses.

S23.

Arrest Record

An arrest is an act depriving a person of his or her liberty rights. A law enforcement agent must have "probable cause" to lawfully arrest a person suspected of committing an offense. This means that a law enforcement agent must have reasonable grounds to believe that the suspect committed the offense.

After an arrest, the suspect is placed in custody and booked or processed. During processing, a law enforcement agent makes an arrest and/or identifying information report, takes a "mugshot" or an ID photo, obtains fingerprints, and performs a criminal history check.

A suspect is then either formally charged with an offense or released without charges being filed. Note that even if the grand jury declines to indict you for a criminal offense or the prosecutor decides not to file charges against you, you will still have record of the arrest. Once the police arrest and fingerprint you, you have a criminal record. You must then expunge your criminal record if you want to make it unavailable for public inspection.

In New Jersey, arrests not resulting in conviction due to Acquittal, Dismissal or Discharge without a conviction or Finding of Guilt are expungeable under the following law and circumstances:

- **Statute:** N.J.S.A. 2C:52-6

- **Waiting Period:** None, statute says "at any time," except for six-month wait required for a Diversion/Supervisory Treatment Program for certain first offenses. See S15.; See also N.J.S.A. 2C:35-36.

CLASSIFICATION OF OFFENSES

- **Other:** If dismissal, discharge, or acquittal resulted from finding of insanity or lack of mental capacity to commit a crime, expungement is not available.

S24.

Young Drug Offender

To qualify for expungement as a Young Drug Offender, a petitioner must be 21 years of age or younger and be convicted of possession or use of a controlled dangerous substance (CDS). Before he or she will be eligible for expungement, a petitioner must wait one year following the conviction, termination of probation or parole or discharge from custody, whichever is later. A petitioner may be granted expungement only if he or she has not violated any conditions of his probation or parole OR committed another crime. In addition, a petitioner must not have obtained dismissal of any charge or conviction due to acceptance into and completion of a supervisory treatment or other diversion program.

Below is an outline of the statutory law and requirements that must be met to expunge a Young Drug Offender conviction under Chapter 35 or 36 of the Title 2C (Comprehensive Drug Reform Act of 1986): [5]

- **Statute:** N.J.S.A. 2C:52-5

- **Waiting Period:** To be eligible for expungement, you must wait one (1) year after, whichever is later:

  a. the date of your conviction,
  b. the termination of your probation or parole, or
  c. your discharge from custody.

- **Other Requirements:**

CLASSIFICATION OF OFFENSES

(1) You must have been 21 years of age or younger at the time you committed the offense.

(2) You must have been convicted of possession or use of a controlled dangerous substance under Chapter 35 or Chapter 36 of New Jersey Law.

(3) You must NOT have been convicted of the sale or distribution of a controlled dangerous substance or possession with the intent to sell any controlled dangerous substance UNLESS your drug conviction was for the sale or distribution of, or possession with intent to sell:

- Marijuana, where the total quantity sold, distributed or possessed with intent to sell was 25 grams or less (approximately 0.88 oz) or

- Hashish, where the total quantity sold, distributed or possessed with intent to sell was 5 grams or less; or (approximately 0.18 oz)

(4) You must not be in violation of your probation or parole.

(5) You must not be convicted of any other indictable offense (crime).

(6) You must not have obtained dismissal of any charge or conviction due to acceptance into and completion of a supervisory treatment or other diversion program.

S25.

Juvenile Adjudication for Delinquency

Delinquency is an act committed by a juvenile under the age of 18 that if committed by an adult would constitute an indictable offense (crime), a disorderly persons offense, a petty disorderly persons offense, or a violation under any other penal statute, ordinance or regulation. When a juvenile commits a criminal offense it is called a juvenile adjudication and not a criminal conviction. Therefore, if a juvenile is found to have committed an offense, the family court can adjudicate him or her, but cannot find him or her guilty of a an offense. However, under New Jersey (Waiver laws) law, if a juvenile is 16 or older, a prosecutor can make a waiver request to transfer the juvenile to an adult court if a public citizen or the like accuses the juvenile of homicide, kidnapping, aggravated assault, and any other violent offenses. Some common juvenile criminal offenses include drug-related offenses, theft and shoplifting, disorderly conduct, assault, alcohol-related offenses ("Baby DWI"), and burglary.

In New Jersey, the Family Court has exclusive jurisdiction over juvenile adjudication matters. When a public citizen or the like accuses a juvenile of a delinquent act, he or she must sign a complaint. The complaint will then be assigned to the Family Court Intake Services for processing. Once the court receives the complaint, the Intake Services Officer, an assistant prosecutor, and a judge will review the complaint to determine the status of the complaint. If the complaint alleges a serious crime, such as homicide, rape, or possession of drugs, it will be delivered to a court judge. However, if the complaint alleges a minor offense, such as shoplifting, disorderly conduct, or stolen property offense, it will be delivered to a Juvenile Conference Committee or an Intake Service Conference.

CLASSIFICATION OF OFFENSES

Adult and Juvenile Comparison Chart

- A juvenile is "taken into custody," while an adult is arrested.

- A juvenile receives an "adjudication of delinquency," while an adult is convicted.

- A juvenile is charged with an offense, while an adult is indicted.

- A juvenile is taken to a juvenile detention center or juvenile justice center, while an adult is taken to jail, prison, or is incarcerated.

- A juvenile receives a "diversion," to a Juvenile Conference Committee or Intake Services Conference, while an adult may receive Pretrial Intervention, Conditional Discharge, or Conditional Dismissal.

Note: In New Jersey, the expungement process is the same for a juvenile record as it is for an adult offense. If you have a juvenile record and an adult record, you should include them both in your expungement petition.

S26.

Juvenile Adjudication & Record Sealing or Expungement

Under New Jersey law, juvenile records are not automatically sealed when a minor reaches the age of 18. In order to prevent public, police, and prosecutor access, a juvenile must petition the court to expunge or seal his or her juvenile record. A juvenile offender may expunge or seal his or her record when he or she reaches the age of 17. A juvenile's ENTIRE record, which includes all delinquent acts while a minor can also be expunged. The purpose of juvenile record sealing or expungement is to provide an opportunity for a juvenile or a minor to have a "clean start," as he or she enters adulthood.

Below is an outline of the types of juvenile offenses or delinquent acts that are eligible for expungement in New Jersey: (N.J.S.A. 2C:52-4.1(a))

1. If act would be an eligible indictable offense if committed by an adult, follow outline and procedure for expungement of indictable offenses (i.e., theft), See S.19.

2. If act would be a disorderly or petty disorderly persons offense if committed by an adult, follow outline and procedure for expungement of disorderly persons offenses and petty disorderly offenses (i.e., simple assault), See S.21.

3. If act would be a municipal ordinance violation if committed by an adult, follow outline and procedure for expungement of municipal ordinance violations (i.e., public urination), See S.22.

CLASSIFICATION OF OFFENSES

> **Note:** All records or convictions are eligible for expungement except those specified as ineligible for expungement if committed by an adult.

To expunge an ENTIRE juvenile adjudication record the following statutes and requirements apply:

- **Statute:** N.J.S.A. 2C:52-4.1, N.J.S.A. 2C:52-2

- **Waiting Period:**

   Your ENTIRE juvenile record may be expunged after five (5) years from final discharge and custody or supervision OR five (5) years have passed after entry of any other court order not involving custody or supervision;

> **Note:** Under old NJ law, a juvenile had to wait five (5) years after he completed his sentence to expunge his juvenile record. Now, under current NJ law, the waiting period begins from the time the juvenile was adjudicated delinquent rather than when he completed his sentence.

- **Other Juvenile Adjudication Requirements:**

   (1) You have never been convicted of an indictable offense, or a disorderly or petty disorderly persons offense, or adjudged a delinquent, or in need of supervision during the 5 years PRIOR to the filing the petition.

   (2) You have never had an adult conviction expunged.

   (3) You have never had adult criminal charges dismissed following completion of a supervisory treatment or other diversion program.

   (4) You have no other proceedings or complaints pending.

S27.

Shoplifting (Theft)

Shoplifting is defined as the willful taking of merchandise from the possession of a store or business establishment with the intent to convert merchandise to one's own use without paying the purchase price.

Under New Jersey law, there are six (6) types of shoplifting offenses: N.J.S.A. 2C:20-11; [1], [29]

1.	**Purposely Taking Merchandise:**	The taking of merchandise from the owner of the store or business with the intent to deprive the merchant of its' benefit or value without paying the purchase price.
2.	**Concealment:**	The hiding or obscuring of merchandise from ordinary observation with the intent to commit a theft.
3.	**Altering or Transferring a Price Tag:**	The altering, removing, or transferring of a price tag with the intent to deprive the merchant of the merchandise without paying the purchase price.

CLASSIFICATION OF OFFENSES

4. **Transferring Merchandise to Another Container:** The transferring of merchandise into a container with intent to commit a theft of the merchandise.

5. **Under–Ringing of Merchandise:** The intentional causing of merchandise to reflect a price lower than the full retail price or value of the merchandise.

6. **Removing a Shopping Cart from the Premises:** The intentional removing of a merchant's shopping cart from the merchant's business premises.

Under New Jersey law, shoplifting offenses are eligible for expungement. If it is your first offense and the judge or jury convicts you of shoplifting merchandise less than $200, a disorderly persons offense, then the court will likely offer you a diversion program, such as Pre-Trial Intervention or Conditional Dismissal. You will then be required to complete probation and/or community service. If it is your first offense and the judge or jury convicts you of a THIRD or FOURTH degree indictable offense, the court will likely offer you Pre-Trial Intervention (PTI) or Conditional Dismissal. When you complete a diversionary program for a disorderly persons offense or an indictable offense, the court will dismiss all charges against you. You will be eligible for expungement six (6) months after the successful completion of the program. If a judge or jury convicts you of shoplifting or theft and you do not enter a diversion program, the general waiting period for a disorderly persons offense and an indictable offense will apply. New Jersey law categorizes shoplifting offenses as follows: (N.J.S.A. 2C:20-11); [1]; [33]

2nd Degree: Shoplifting is a crime of the second degree if the full retail value of the merchandise was $75,000.00 or more. N.J.S.A. 2C:20-11c(1). A crime of the second degree is punishable by a term of imprisonment of five to 10 years (N.J.S.A. 2C:43-6a(2)), a fine not to exceed $150,000.00, or both (N.J.S.A. 2C:43-3a(2)).

3rd Degree:

Shoplifting is a crime of the third degree if the full retail value of the merchandise exceeds $500.00 but is less than $75,000.00. N.J.S.A. 2C:20-11c(2). A crime of the third degree is punishable by a term of imprisonment of three to five years (N.J.S.A. 2C:43-6a(3)), a fine not to exceed $15,000.00, or both (N.J.S.A. 2C:43-3b(1)).

4th Degree:

Shoplifting is a crime of the fourth degree if the full retail value of the merchandise was at least $200.00 but does not exceed $500.00. N.J.S.A. 2C:20-11c(3). A crime of the fourth degree is punishable by a term of imprisonment not to exceed 18 months (N.J.S.A. 2C:43-6a(4)), a fine not to exceed $10,000, or both (N.J.S.A. 2C:43-3b(2)).

Disorderly Persons Offense:

Shoplifting is a disorderly persons offense if the full retail value of the merchandise was less than $200.00. N.J.S.A. 2C:20-11c(4). A disorderly persons offense is punishable by a term of imprisonment not to exceed six months (N.J.S.A. 2C:43-8), a fine not to exceed $1,000, or both (N.J.S.A. 2C:43-3c).

The additional mandatory penalties for any person convicted of a shoplifting offense under the Act are as follows:

Additional Mandatory Penalties:

For a first offense, at least ten days of community service; for a second offense,

97

at least 15 days of community service; and for a third or subsequent offense, a maximum of 25 days of community service; and any person convicted of a third or subsequent shoplifting offense shall serve a minimum term of imprisonment of not less than 90 days. N.J.S.A. 2C:20-11c(4).

S28.

Possession & Distribution of Drugs

What is the difference between drug possession and drug distribution, as it relates to expungement eligibility?

In New Jersey, drug possession convictions are generally expungeable. Drug selling or distribution convictions are generally non-expungeable, unless your conviction qualifies for expungement under one (1) of New Jersey's three (3) exceptions. You are eligible for expungement if your conviction is for the selling of 25 grams or less of marijuana, 5 grams or less of hash, or any controlled dangerous substance (CDS) where the conviction is of the THIRD or FOURTH degree. N.J.S.A. 2C:52-2 Note: Possession of larger quantities of a drug can lead to charges of "possession with intent to sell."

Are drug possession convictions eligible for expungement?

Yes. Under New Jersey law, marijuana POSSESSION convictions are generally eligible for expungement. If you are a first-time drug offender, the court will likely offer you a diversion program, such as Pre-Trial Intervention (PTI). After the successful completion of the Pre-Trial Intervention program, the court will dismiss the conviction. However, there will still be a public record of your arrest that will be searchable by an employer or the like performing a background check. To prevent your arrest or drug charge from being publicly searchable, you must apply for expungement. In New Jersey, you may apply for expungement after six (6) months of completing the diversion program. If you do not complete or were not granted a diversion program, you must wait five (5) years to expunge your drug possession conviction.

CLASSIFICATION OF OFFENSES

Are drug distribution and possession of drugs with the intent to sell convictions eligible for expungement?

Yes, in certain cases. Convictions for drug distribution and possession of drugs with the intent to sell are eligible for expungement in New Jersey under the following conditions:

1. Marijuana, where the total quantity sold, distributed or possessed with intent to sell was 25 grams or less (approximately 0.88 oz);

2. Hashish, where the total quantity sold, distributed or possessed with intent to sell was 5 grams or less (approximately 0.18 oz); or

3. Any controlled dangerous substance (CDS) such as cocaine, heroin, or ecstasy, provided that the conviction is of the THIRD or FOURTH degree, where the court finds that expungement is consistent with the PUBLIC INTEREST, giving due consideration to the nature of the offense and the petitioner's character and conduct since conviction. In such cases, the court must consider whether the need for the availability of the records outweighs the petitioner's interest in expunging the records.

Are convictions for conspiracy to possess, distribute, or sell CDS eligible for expungement?

Yes. Convictions for conspiracy to possess, distribute, or sell CDS may also be eligible for expungement. See In re R.W.B., 2010 WL 1740904, [18]; But see In re D.A.C., 337 N.J. Super. 493 (App.Div. 2001) holding that accomplices are barred from expungement (overruling Application of R.C., 292 N.J. Super. 151 (Law Div. 1996)

Note: If you have a drug distribution or possession with the intent to sell conviction, a prosecutor is likely to object to your petition for expungement. You will have to attend an in-court hearing if a prosecutor or government agency objects.

CLASSIFICATION OF OFFENSES

Note: Under New Jersey law, a conviction for the sale or distribution of a controlled dangerous substance or possession with intent to sell in the THIRD or FOURTH degree is eligible for expungement. However, a conviction for the sale or distribution of a controlled dangerous substance or possession with intent to sell in the FIRST or SECOND degree is not eligible for expungement.

Below is a chart outlining statutory law governing the possession and distribution of marijuana and hash in New Jersey. N.J.S.A. 2C:35-10; [5]

Marijuana Possession

Amount:	Offense:	Sentence:	Max. Fine
50 g or less	Disorderly Persons	6 months	$1,000
More than 50 g	Indictable Offense (4th Degree)	1.5 years	$25,000

Marijuana Distribution, Possession with Intent to Distribute, or Cultivation

Amount:	Offense:	Sentence:	Max. Fine
Less than 1 oz	Indictable Offense	1.5 years	$ 25,000
1 oz - 5 lbs	Indictable Offense	3 - 5 years	$ 25,000
25 lbs or more	Indictable Offense	10 - 20 years	$ 300,000

CLASSIFICATION OF OFFENSES

Hash Possession & Distribution

Amount:	Offense:	Sentence:	Max. Fine
Possession	Disorderly Persons	6 months	$ 1,000
Manufacturing, distributing, selling, or possessing with intent of less than 5 g	Indictable Offense (4th Degree)	18 months	$ 10,000
Manufacturing, distributing, selling, or possessing with intent of 5 g - 1lb	Indictable Offense (3rd Degree)	5 years	$ 15,000
Manufacturing, distributing, selling, or possessing with intent of 1 lb – 5 lbs	Indictable Offense (2nd Degree)	10 years	$ 150,000
Manufacturing, distributing, selling, or possessing with intent of 5 lbs or more	Indictable Offense (1st Degree)	20 years	$ 200,000

S29.

Non-Expungeable Indictable Offenses

Refer to S.19 for a list of indictable offenses or crimes that can never be expunged.

S30.

Grounds for Denial of Expungement Relief

Refer to S.3 for a list of general reasons a judge may deny your petition for expungement in New Jersey.

S31.

Out-of-State Convictions

Should I List My Out-of-State Conviction(s) On My Petition for Expungement in New Jersey?

Yes. New Jersey counts convictions from another state toward the maximum number of convictions a petitioner must not exceed to expunge his or her record. If you are not sure about whether you have an out-of-state conviction, you should get a copy your criminal history record from the FBI. See S5. The New Jersey courts will compare the out-of-state conviction to the New Jersey conviction to determine how it will classify the out-of-state conviction. The court, in its discretion, may decide to treat the out-of-state felony as a disorderly persons offense in New Jersey or vice versa. However, for sentencing purposes N.J.S.A. 2C:44-4c provides that a "conviction in another jurisdiction shall constitute a prior conviction of crime if a sentence of imprisonment in excess of 6 months was authorized under the law of the other jurisdiction." [1]; [29]

S32.

Plea Bargain

If a prosecutor dismisses charges against you as a result of a plea bargain in which you agreed to a conviction on other charge(s), you must first expunge the conviction(s) before you can expunge the dismissed charges. Thus, the waiting period requirement may change for each charge depending on the level of the offense.

Example:

Niklaus is charged with 1 disorderly persons offense + 1 indictable offense. Niklaus pleads guilty to the indictable offense charge in exchange for the disorderly persons offense being dismissed. (plea bargain) Before Niklaus can expunge his ARREST for the disorderly persons offense, he must expunge the indictable conviction. The waiting time required for the indictable conviction is ten (10) years, unless Niklaus qualifies for "early pathway," in which he can apply for expungement after five (5) years from the date of conviction, payment of fines, satisfactory completion of probation or parole, or release from incarceration, WHICHEVER IS LATER. See S15.; S16.; S.33. Therefore, if Niklaus qualifies for "early pathway" for his indictable conviction, he must wait five (5) years from the date of conviction, payment of fines, satisfactory completion of probation or parole, or release from incarceration, WHICHEVER IS LATER, to expunge his ARREST for the disorderly persons offense. See S15.; S16.; S33. If Nicklaus does not qualify for "early pathway" he must wait ten (10) years from the date of conviction, payment of fines, satisfactory completion of probation or parole, or release from incarceration, WHICHEVER IS LATER, to expunge his ARREST for the disorderly persons offense. See S15.; S16.

S33.

Early Pathway Case

"Early pathway" refers to the court's discretion to expunge an indictable offense before the statutory 10-year time requirement. "Early pathway" provides an exception to the 10-year requirement and grants a petitioner two (2) options to expunge his or her conviction in less than 10 years. New Jersey law permits expungement before the 10-year waiting requirement if: N.J.S.A. 2C:52–2a(2); [1]; [4]

1. less than TEN (10) years has expired from the satisfaction of a fine, but the 10-year time requirement is otherwise satisfied, and the court finds that the person substantially complied with any payment plan ordered pursuant to N.J.S.2C:46-1 et seq., or could not do so due to compelling circumstances affecting his ability to satisfy the fine; or

2. at least FIVE (5) years has expired from the date of his conviction, payment of fine, satisfactory completion of probation or parole, or release from incarceration, whichever is later; the person has not been convicted of a crime, disorderly persons offense, or petty disorderly persons offense since the time of the conviction; and the court finds in its discretion that expungement is in the PUBLIC INTEREST giving due consideration to the nature of the offense and the applicant's character and conduct since conviction. See In re Ronald C. Kollman, Jr., Petition for Expungement (A-126-10)(067807); [16]

CLASSIFICATION OF OFFENSES

What does this mean?

Under N.J.S.A. 2C:52–2a(2), you can expunge your conviction in FIVE (5) years, if you can prove it is in the public interest.

Before the recent amendment, the New Jersey Criminal Code required applicants to wait ten (10) years before petitioning the court to expunge their conviction for an indictable offense. Now, you can apply sooner than ten (10) years if:

1. you have not had any new convictions since your original offense;

2. at least five years have passed since satisfaction of all sentence obligations (e.g., parole, probation, fines); and

3. the court finds that granting your petition is in the public interest. (The court must consider the nature of your offense and your character and conduct since conviction)

While the first two requirements are clear, courts may use their discretion in determining the third. The court will also consider the third prong if you are expunging a third or fourth degree drug sale or distribution conviction.

> **Note:** If you have an "early pathway" case, a prosecutor is likely to object. If a prosecutor or government agency objects to your petition for expungement, you will have to attend an in-court hearing. A court may consider any facts or evidence surrounding the circumstances of the arrest to determine your "character and conduct since the conviction." See In re Lobasso, 423 N.J. Super. 475 (App. Div. 2012); [14]. See also State v. Merendino, 293 NJ Super. 444 (App.Div. 1996) (Use of extraneous facts related to arrest to bar expungement); [17].

S34.

Mental Health Records

Can I expunge a mental health record?

Yes. Under N.J.S. 30:4-80.11, if the Superior Court of New Jersey grants your petition for expungement for a mental health commitment, New Jersey treats the commitment as if it never occurred. You may then legally answer "no" to any questions related to you having a mental health record. In effect, the county court(s) and applicable government agencies will extract and isolate your mental health record. [30]

Am I eligible to expunge my mental health record?

Generally, under N.J.S. 30:4-80.8, you may petition the Superior Court for expungement of your mental health commitment if you were:

1. committed by order of any court or by voluntary commitment to an institution or facility providing mental health services; and

2. discharged or determined to be recovered, substantially improved, or substantially in remission. [30]

Can I lawfully possess a firearm if I have expunged my mental health record?

Yes. Generally, New Jersey law prohibits a person committed due to a mental illness from legally possessing a firearm or obtaining a license to own a firearm.

CLASSIFICATION OF OFFENSES

N.J.S. 2C:58-3(c)(3); N.J.S. 2C:39-7(6)(a); [31]; [29]. However, expungement of your mental health commitment will remove the commitment and disqualification and allow you to obtain a license to own a firearm.

> **Note:** Unlike applicants who are legally required to reveal their expunged CRIMINAL RECORD when applying for a job with a law enforcement agency or corrections, applicants who have expunged their MENTAL HEALTH RECORD are not required to do so. However, applicants who have expunged their MENTAL HEALTH RECORD are legally required to reveal their expunged mental health record when applying for a job with the courts or judicial system.

S35.

Public Interest Case

If you have a "public interest" case, a prosecutor or government agency is likely to object to your petition for expungement. If a prosecutor or government agency objects to your petition for expungement, you will have to attend an in-court hearing. A Superior Court judge must then decide whether "the need for the availability of records outweighs the desirability of expungement." See In Re Ronald C. Kollman, Jr., Petition for Expungement (A-126-10) (067807); [16] The judge will analyze a number of factors to determine if he or she will grant you an Order of Expungement. Factors such as your "character and conduct subsequent to conviction" and the "nature of your conviction" will be heavily weighed by the court. See In Re Ronald C. Kollman; [16]

If you choose to represent yourself in court in a "public interest" case, you must draft additional paperwork to adequately prepare for your case. You cannot use the basic expungement packet prepared by the New Jersey Judiciary to prepare for and successfully argue a "public interest" case in court. Public interest cases are more complex and require a greater understanding of New Jersey expungement law. You must gather and organize several additional documents including, but not limited to, a character statement, a work history and resume, letters of personal and professional reference, and vocational and license certificates. In "In Re Ronald C. Kollman, Jr.", Mr. Kollman submitted 21 reference letters along with his application attesting to his moral character, accomplishments, good deeds, and personal growth to support his application for expungement.

CLASSIFICATION OF OFFENSES

In "In Re Ronald C. Kollman, Jr.," Petition for Expungement (A-126-10) (067807)," the court stipulated the following: [16]

> To decide whether expungement is in the public interest, courts consider the NATURE OF THE OFFENSE and the applicant's CHARACTER AND CONDUCT SINCE THE CONVICTION. Courts will also consider whether the need for the availability of records outweighs the desirability of expungement. The defendant seeking an expungement has the burden of demonstrating, by a preponderance of the evidence, why expungement would be in the public interest. If the State objects on statutory grounds, the burden of proof shifts to the State.
>
> To determine the NATURE OF THE OFFENSE, a court may review the undisputed or proven facts about the crime and its commission, including the definition, grade, and elements of an offense. A judge may also consider what the petitioner did, how and with whom he acted, the harm he/she may have caused, and any related charges that have been dismissed if the underlying facts have been substantiated or are undisputed. To assist the court, a petitioner must include with his petition plea agreements, trial and sentencing agreements, and pre-sentence reports, if available.

The court, as stated in "In Re Ronald Kollman," must weigh several factors in deciding whether to accept or deny a petition for expungement. [16] In "New Jersey's Supreme Court Provides Guidance in Filing Public Interest Expungements" article in the November 2012 edition of "Looking Out for Your Legal Rights" at the Legal Services of New Jersey (LSNJ) website, LSNJ duly noted that the court cannot deny an application for expungement simply because the petitioner is deemed to have committed a serious offense. [22]; [23]

CLASSIFICATION OF OFFENSES

In considering the NATURE OF THE OFFENSE, the court may not impose a "categorical" or generic denial. This means that the court cannot deny your application simply because it considers a certain type of offense "serious." It must fairly consider any evidence of rehabilitation you provide. (*LSNJ LAW Website, 9-10)*; [22]; [23]; [See 16]

To evaluate the CHARACTER AND CONDUCT SINCE THE CONVICTION, the courts may consider established or undisputed facts, not unproven allegations, that a petitioner has been rehabilitated since his/her conviction, including: [22]

- Your behavior and performance while in jail and on probation or parole;

- Your activities that either enhanced or limited the risk of re-offending;

- Facts relating to a dismissed charge or arrest that did not result in a conviction;

- Your conduct before the time of the conviction to gauge whether the offense was aberrational;

- Your family and community ties;

- Your education and vocation;

- Your satisfaction of fines and other legal obligations; and

- Your distance from the criminal element (physical, mental).

(*LSNJ LAW Website, 9-10)*

"You must submit a written statement with your public interest petition along with any evidence you have that explains the nature of your offense, and your character and conduct since your conviction. You should try to submit as much positive evidence as possible," such as: [22]; [See 16]

<u>CLASSIFICATION OF OFFENSES</u>

- Diplomas, GED, or other educational and vocational certificates and licenses

- Work history and resumes

- Letters of personal and professional reference

- Documents showing that you have paid or otherwise met all of your legal obligations

    (LSNJ LAW Website, 9-10)

What will the court look for specifically?

The nature of the offense you committed: [See 16]

- Was the offense violent or non-violent?

- Were you a juvenile or an adult?

- How serious was the offense? (What was the degree of the offense?)

- Did the crime involve a victim?

- Were your acts intentional or a mistake?

- Did your acts involve dishonesty?

Your character:

- Are you remorseful?

- Have you accepted responsibility for your past conduct?

- Have you "turned your life around?"

- What are your plans for the future?

CLASSIFICATION OF OFFENSES

Your conduct since your conviction:

- Any other convictions (before or after)?

- What is your education?

- Are you employed? Seeking employment?

- Have you attended drug/alcohol rehab?

- What is your religious membership and activity, if any?

- What are your family connections?

- Have you received any letters of support, educational /vocational certificates, awards, or recognitions?

(LSNJ LAW Website, 9-10)

S36.

Public Office

If a person holding public office commits a crime that involves or touches his or her position as a public official, he or she is not eligible for expungement. Such relief cannot be granted if the crime directly relates to, flows from, or involves the person's office, position, or employment as a public employee.

> Records of conviction for any crime committed by a person holding any public office, position or employment, elective or appointive, under the government of this State or any agency or political subdivision thereof and any conspiracy or attempt to commit such a crime shall not be subject to expungement if the crime involved or touched such office, position or employment. N.J.S.A. 2C:52-2b; [1]

S37.

Physician or Podiatrist Involving Drugs & Alcohol

If a state physician or podiatrist is convicted of an offense involving drugs or alcohol, the court must inform the State Board of Medical Examiners of his or her petition for expungement.

> In the case of a State licensed physician or podiatrist convicted of an offense involving drugs or alcohol or pursuant to section 14 or 15 of P.L.1989, c.300 (C.2C:21-20 or 2C:21-4.1), the court shall notify the State Board of Medical Examiners upon receipt of a petition for expungement of the conviction and records and information pertaining thereto. N.J.S.A. 2C:52-2d; [1]

S38.

DUI

In many states, Driving Under the Influence (DUI) is a criminal offense; however, in New Jersey it is not. Under Chapter 4 of Title 39 of the New Jersey Motor Vehicles and Traffic Regulation Code, a DUI is a motor vehicle offense. [4] You cannot expunge a motor vehicle conviction in New Jersey, which includes driving under the influence of alcohol or drugs. However, if the State of New Jersey convicts you of a DUI, and a potential employer asks you on a job application whether you have ever been convicted of a crime, you may truthfully answer "no" to the question without any legal repercussions. [2]; [4]

Note: In New Jersey, the municipal courts have authority over motor vehicle offense cases.

S39.

Federal Offenses

Generally, expungement is not available for federal offenses. However, there is one exception to the rule.

Under Title 18, Section 3607 of the United States Code, a provision exists for persons who obtain a "Special Probation" to expunge a federal conviction for simple possession of controlled substances. The section applies to persons who:

- are charged with simple possession of controlled dangerous substances;

- are under 21 years of age at the time of the offense; and

- do not have a prior conviction for a drug offense.

Generally, you have to prove that the conviction was wrongful or unconstitutional.

In addition, the U.S. Supreme Court has yet to decide whether a person charged in a federal criminal complaint with violating a state statute on federal property can expunge his or her criminal record. Also, the federal circuit courts are split as to whether federal courts have the authority to expunge criminal records. The U.S. Supreme Court has yet to rule on the matter; and on two occasions, the Supreme Court has declined requests for certiorari.

However, if you do not qualify for "Special Probation," you can apply for a pardon through the President of the United States.

S40.

Restraining Orders

A restraining order is a civil no-contact order and not a criminal offense. A criminal record will not list a restraining order. A restraining order is not eligible for expungement in New Jersey. Note that although a restraining order is not a criminal offense, violating a restraining order is a criminal offense. Under N.J.S. 2C:29-9: [4]

Contempt

a. A person is guilty of a crime of the fourth degree if he purposely or knowingly disobeys a judicial order or hinders, obstructs or impedes the effectuation of a judicial order or the exercise of jurisdiction over any person, thing or controversy by a court, administrative body or investigative entity.

b. Except as provided below, a person is guilty of a crime of the fourth degree if that person purposely or knowingly violates any provision in an order entered under the provisions of the "Prevention of Domestic Violence Act of 1991," P.L. 1991, c.261 (C. 2C:25-17 et al.) when the conduct which constitutes the violation could also constitute a crime or a disorderly persons offense. In all other cases a person is guilty of a disorderly persons offense if that person knowingly violates an order entered under the provisions of this act. Orders entered pursuant to paragraphs (3), (4), (5), (8) and (9) of subsection b. of section 13 of P.L. 1991, c.261 (C. 2C:25-29) shall be excluded from the provisions of this subsection.

S41.

Can I Expunge a Criminal Record from Another State in New Jersey?

No. You can only expunge New Jersey arrest(s) and/or conviction(s) in New Jersey. You cannot combine arrest(s) and/or conviction(s) from different states and expunge them in one state. You must expunge your arrest(s) and/or conviction(s) in the state where your arrest and/or prosecution occurred. Therefore, you should seek legal advice from a competent attorney in the state where your arrest(s) and/or conviction(s) occurred.

S42.

Personnel Records Containing Expunged Criminal Records in Employment Files

Personnel records containing expunged criminal records in employment files cannot be removed. The effect of the expungement is to preclude "all records on file within any court, detention or correctional facility, law enforcement or criminal justice agency concerning a person's detection, apprehension, arrest, detention, trial or disposition of an offense within the criminal justice system ...[,]" from being publicly searchable. N.J.S.A. 2C:52-1(a); [1] As stated in State v. Zemak, "the issue at bar is not whether the order for expungement should be granted, but whether or not the expungement statute controls petitioner's personnel records as maintained by the Secaucus Police Department." 304 N.J. Super. 381 (App.Div. 1997); [15].

Are personnel records containing expunged criminal records in employment files beyond the reach of N.J.S.A. 2C:52-1(a)?

Yes. In E.A. v. New Jersey Real Estate Com'n, the Appellate Division held that state agencies other than law enforcement are beyond the expungement statute and cannot be compelled to remove references from their records. 208 N.J.Super. 65, 504 A.2d 1213 (App.Div.), certif. den. 104 N.J. 415, 517 A.2d 413 (1986); See State v. Zemak 304 N.J. Super. 381 (App.Div. 1997); [15]. In State v. Zemak, the court expanded the coverage or limitation to include the Police Department as an employer. 304 N.J. Super. 381 (App.Div. 1997); [15]

CLASSIFICATION OF OFFENSES

The statute governing the expungement of records does not subject the Police Department as employer to the same restrictions as it does the Police Department as law enforcement entity. The purpose of the statute is to provide relief to the "one-time offender" and allow him to carry on as if the proceedings never occurred. However, in light of the Secaucus Police Department's duty to ensure public safety, and therefore maintain complete performance records of all its employees, the need for the availability of those personnel records outweighs the desirability of having them isolated. State v. Zemak 304 N.J. Super. 385 (App.Div. 1997); [15]

S43.

Domestic Violence

What is domestic violence?

Domestic violence is not a crime per se. There is no law which provides for a domestic law conviction. However, domestic violence is a term used to categorize certain crimes carried out against a person protected by the New Jersey Prevention of Domestic Violence Act of 1991 (PDVA). The definition of domestic violence varies between states.

Whether a crime is domestic violence in New Jersey depends on the type of crime and the nature of the victim. To qualify as domestic violence, the assailant must carry out the crime against a person protected by the PDVA. In New Jersey, domestic violence involves violence or threat of violence, abuse or harassment against a spouse, former spouse, any present or former member of the same household, someone in a dating relationship, or someone who has, or is about to have a child in common.

CLASSIFICATION OF OFFENSES

> **Domestic Violence is governed by Chapter 25 of Title 2C of the New Jersey Code of Criminal Justice. In New Jersey, there are fourteen (14) types of crimes that apply to a person protected under the PDVA: [6]**

Homicide	N.J.S.A. 2C:11-1
Assault	N.J.S.A. 2C:12-1
Terroristic threats	N.J.S.A. 2C:12-3
Kidnapping	N.J.S.A. 2C:13-1
Criminal restraint	N.J.S.A. 2C:13-2
False imprisonment	N.J.S.A. 2C:13-3
Sexual assault	N.J.S.A. 2C:14-2
Criminal sexual contact.	N.J.S.A. 2C:14-3
Lewdness	N.J.S.A. 2C:14-4
Criminal mischief.	N.J.S.A. 2C:17-3
Burglary	N.J.S.A. 2C:18-2
Criminal trespass	N.J.S.A. 2C:18-3
Harassment	N.J.S.A. 2C:33-4
Stalking	N.J.S.A. 2C:12-10

Are all fourteen (14) crimes expungeable?

1. Homicide and kidnapping are never eligible for expungement.

2. Criminal restraint (if the victim is a minor and the offender is not the parent), false imprisonment (if the victim is minor and the offender is not the parent), sexual assault (if aggravated), and criminal sexual contact (if victim is a minor) are occasionally expunged.

3. Assault, terroristic threats, lewdness, criminal mischief, burglary, criminal trespass, harassment, and stalking are frequently expunged.

4. A dismissed charge is always and immediately expungeable.

Who qualifies as a protected person in New Jersey?

1. A protected person includes any person:

- who is 18 years of age or older, or

- who is an emancipated minor, and who has been subjected to domestic violence by:

    - a spouse,

    - a former spouse, or

    - any other person who is a present or former household member.

2. A protected person is a person, who regardless of age, has been subjected to domestic violence by a person:

    - with whom the victim has had a child in common, or

    - with whom the victim anticipates on having a child in common.

3. A protected person is a person, who regardless of age, has been subjected to domestic violence by a person with whom the victim has had a dating relationship.

    - the domestic violence assailant must be over the age of 18 **OR** EMANCIPATED at the time of the offense.

        - A minor is considered EMANCIPATED from his or her parents when the minor:

            - has been married,

            - has entered the military service,

            - has a child or is pregnant, or

            - has been previously declared by a court or an administrative agency to be emancipated.

CLASSIFICATION OF OFFENSES

Note: In many cases, the court will dismiss a domestic violence charge in exchange for participation in an anger management or other similar program. The most common dismissed charge is simple assault.

S44.

Crime Spree Doctrine

Generally, if you have more than one (1) indictable offense conviction, you are not eligible to expunge any of your convictions. However, you may qualify for expungement if your multiple indictable convictions arise out of a common scheme or criminal spree. State v. Fontana, 146 N.J. Super. 264 (app. Div. 1976); [11]. But see State v. Ross, 400 N.J. Super. 117 (App. Div. 2008) N.J.S.A. 2C:52-2(a); [12]

CHAPTER 4

MULTIPLE CONVICTIONS

S45.

Are Multiple Convictions Expungeable?

REMINDER:

There are four (4) general categories of offenses that are eligible for expungement in New Jersey:

1.	Indictable Offenses / Crimes
2.	Disorderly Persons Offenses or Petty Disorderly Persons Offenses
3.	Municipal Ordinance Violations
4.	Motor Vehicle or Traffic Offenses

In New Jersey, when determining whether a criminal record with multiple convictions is eligible for expungement, the court will take in consideration the type and number of offenses the petitioner has committed. If a petitioner has multiple convictions, the court will determine which convictions, if any, qualify for expungement. The courts refer to Chapter 52 of Title 2C of the New Jersey Code of Criminal Justice which specifies the type and number of offenses that are eligible for expungement. There are many combinations to consider when evaluating expungement eligibility for multiple convictions.

MULTIPLE CONVICTIONS

For multiple convictions, use the chart below to determine the type and number of conviction combinations that are eligible for expungement.

Multiple Convictions / Expungement Eligibility Chart	
Indictable Offenses / Crimes	One (1) conviction may be expunged provided petitioner has not been convicted of any other indictable offense or more than two (2) disorderly persons offenses.
Disorderly Persons Offenses (Including Petty Disorderly Persons Offenses)	Up to three (3) convictions may be expunged provided petitioner has not been convicted of an indictable offense.
Municipal Ordinance Violations	No limit provided petitioner has not been convicted of an indictable offense or more than two (2) disorderly persons offenses.
Juvenile Delinquency Offenses	All records or convictions are eligible for expungement except those specified as ineligible for expungement if committed by an adult.
Records of Young Drug Offenders	No limit if conviction is for POSSESSION or USE of CDS
Arrests Not Resulting in Conviction	No Limit

MULTIPLE CONVICTIONS

Example 1:

If a jury convicts Nucky of burglary and a sex crime, both considered indictable offenses under New Jersey law, neither conviction will be eligible for expungement. However, Nucky may expunge any arrests that did not result in a conviction. Reason: Under New Jersey law, a petitioner can expunge no more than one (1) indictable conviction. If he or she has more than one (1) indictable conviction, each conviction is no longer eligible for expungement.

Note: You cannot expunge an indictable conviction, a disorderly persons conviction, or a municipal ordinance violation if you have another indictable conviction or more than three (3) disorderly persons convictions.

Example 2:

1 Indictable Offense + 1 to 2 Disorderly Persons Offenses = 1 Expungeable Indictable Offense and NO Expungeable Disorderly Persons Offenses.

Example 3:

3 Disorderly Persons Offenses + 1$^+$ Municipal Ordinance Violations = 3 Expungeable Disorderly Persons Offenses and NO Expungeable Municipal Ordinance Violations.

REMINDER:

Your expungement eligibility can quickly be determined by taking what we, at the Law Firm of Vonnie C. Dones III, ESQ., call the smelly New Jersey "FEET." "FEET" stands for Free Expungement Eligibility Test, and of course, we offer "FEET" for our prospective clients at www.legalcleanup.com. Based on your answer selections, the test automatically figures out whether you are eligible to expunge your conviction(s).

CHAPTER 5

DIVERSION / SUPERVISORY TREATMENT PROGRAMS

S46.

Diversion Program

The New Jersey Diversion program is a probationary program designed for first time offenders. The purpose of the program is to allow first time offenders an opportunity to get their lives back on track without having the stigma of a criminal conviction on his or her record. Defendants avoid ordinary prosecution by receiving early rehabilitative services. The program aims to deter future criminal behavior. Once a defendant successfully completes diversionary probation the court will dismiss the charges against the defendant. If the court sentences you to a diversion program, such as Conditional Discharge, Pretrial Intervention, Conditional Dismissal, Juvenile Conference Committee, Intake Service Conference, or a Deferred Disposition, and subsequently dismisses the charges against you, then you may have your arrest expunged 6 months after entry of the dismissal order. Outlined below is a summary of the waiting period requirements:

- **Statute:** N.J.S.A. 2C:52-6(b)

- **Waiting Period:** If you successfully complete a diversion program you may have your arrest expunged 6 months after entry of the order of dismissal according to N.J.S.A. 2C:52-6(b); See S15.

Note: It is important to consult a competent New Jersey attorney about the options you may have regarding a prosecutor's decision to "take the case in" or to "downgrade." Such a decision can have a profound effect on the outcome of your case.

DIVERSION / SUPERVISORY TREATMENT PROGRAM

Generally, New Jersey has four (4) types of adult diversion programs, namely Pretrial Intervention (PTI), Conditional Discharge, Conditional Dismissal, and Deferred Disposition / Diversion. Each program serves the same purpose; but each program has different eligibility requirements.

Note: If the court dismissed your case or you successfully completed a diversion program, your criminal record will not show a conviction for the dismissed offense. However, you are still required to list all of your offenses on your petition for expungement, including any offense the court dismissed due to your participation in a diversion program.

S47.

Pretrial Intervention (PTI)

Pretrial Intervention (PTI) is a diversion program that permits the dismissal of a criminal offense by successfully completing a period of supervision (e.g. probation). In New Jersey, N.J.S.A. 2C:43-12 and -13 and Court Rule 3:28 establishes the PTI program. Once the court admits you into the program, it suspends the complaint and/or proceedings against you until the end of your probationary term, which by law, cannot exceed thirty-six (36) months. When you successfully complete the conditions or probationary requirements of the PTI, the court will enter an order for dismissal, dismissing the charge(s). After the court dismisses the charge(s) against you, you can then apply for expungement under N.J.S.A. 2C:52-6. If you successfully complete the conditions or probationary requirements of the PTI, you may have your arrest expunged 6 months after entry of the order of dismissal according to N.J.S.A. 2C:52-6(b). See S15.

The New Jersey legislature designed Pretrial Intervention (PTI) to service individuals charged with THIRD or FOURTH Degree indictable offenses.

Note: Persons charged with offenses involving the sale, distribution, or possession of CDS with intent to distribute Schedule I or II drugs are not eligible for Pretrial Intervention, unless the prosecutor consents.

Below is a summary of the Pretrial Intervention (PTI) program: [32]

- **Statute:** N.J.S.A. 2C:43-12 and -13

- **Court Rule:** 3:28

DIVERSION / SUPERVISORY TREATMENT PROGRAM

- **Limitations:** Indictable Offenses (crimes)

- **Eligibility:** A defendant is eligible for Pretrial Intervention (PTI) if he or she:

  (1) is 18 years of age or older (or juveniles between the ages of 14 and 18 the courts elect to treat as adults under R. 5:22-1 or 5:22-1);

  (2) is a New Jersey resident (ineligible if you reside such distances from New Jersey as to bar effective counseling or supervisory procedures);

  (3) has been charged with a THIRD Degree or FOURTH Degree crime;

  (4) has not completed probation, incarceration, or parole within the last 5 years;

  (5) has never had the benefit of participation in a diversion program previously; and

  (6) has been charged with an offense that does not involve the sale, distribution, or possession of CDS with intent to distribute Schedule I or II drugs.

- **Purposes of PTI:** Guideline 1 of the "Guidelines for Operation Of Pretrial Intervention In New Jersey." (As Amended Effective September 4, 2012)

  (a) To provide defendants with opportunities to avoid ordinary prosecution by receiving early rehabilitative services, when such services can reasonably be expected to deter future criminal behavior by the defendant, and when there is an apparent causal connection between the offense charged and the rehabilitative need, without which cause both the alleged offense and the need to prosecute might not have occurred.

  (b) To provide an alternative to prosecution for defendants who might be harmed by the imposition of criminal sanctions as presently administered, when such an alternative can be expected to serve as sufficient sanction to deter criminal conduct.

(c) To provide a mechanism for permitting the least burdensome form of prosecution possible for defendants charged with "victimless" offenses.

(d) To assist in the relief of presently overburdened criminal calendars in order to focus expenditure of criminal justice resources on matters involving serious criminality and severe correctional problems.

(e) To deter future criminal or disorderly behavior by a defendant/participant in pretrial intervention. (Guideline 1)

- **Time to Apply:** The applicant must file the application no later than 28 days of Indictment.

- **Length of Probation:** Up to thirty-six (36) months. Typically twelve (12) months.

- **Waiting Period:** Six (6) months after entry of the dismissal order.

- **First Degree, Second Degree & Drug Distribution Crimes:** First Degree, Second Degree, and Drug Distribution indictable offenses (crimes) involving a Schedule I or Schedule II form of CDS are not eligible for PTI, unless the prosecutor consents.

- **Other Crimes Not Eligible for Acceptance into PTI:** Under Pretrial Intervention Guideline 3, certain crimes are not eligible for acceptance into PTI such as: (1) organized criminal activity; (2) continuing criminal business or enterprise; (3) those involving violent crime against another person; (4) breach of public trust; and (5) school zone drug distribution.

- **Disorderly Persons Offenses:** Each county, at its' own discretion, may determine whether it will admit the defendant into the PTI program for disorderly persons or petty disorderly persons charges. The county where the offense is pending has exclusive authority in determining whether to admit a defendant into the PTI program.

- **Factors in Evaluating Whether the Court Should Admit an Eligible Candidate into PTI:** N.J.S.A. 2C:43-12(e)

DIVERSION / SUPERVISORY TREATMENT PROGRAM

(1) The nature of the offense;

(2) The facts of the case;

(3) The motivation and age of the defendant;

(4) The desire of the complainant or victim to forego prosecution;

(5) The existence of personal problems and character traits which may be related to the applicant's crime and for which services are unavailable within the criminal justice system, or which may be provided more effectively through supervisory treatment and the probability that the causes of criminal behavior can be controlled by proper treatment;

(6) The likelihood that the applicant's crime is related to a condition or situation that would be conducive to change through his participation in supervisory treatment;

(7) The needs and interests of the victim and society;

(8) The extent to which the applicant's crime constitutes part of a continuing pattern of anti-social behavior;

(9) The applicant's record of criminal and penal violations and the extent to which he may present a substantial danger to others;

(10) Whether or not the crime is of an assaultive or violent nature, whether in the criminal act itself or in the possible injurious consequences of such behavior;

(11) Consideration of whether or not prosecution would exacerbate the social problem that led to the applicant's criminal act;

(12) The history of the use of physical violence toward others;

(13) Any involvement of the applicant with organized crime;

(14) Whether or not the crime is of such a nature that the value of supervisory treatment would be outweighed by the public need for

prosecution;

(15) Whether or not the applicant's involvement with other people in the crime charged or in other crime is such that the interest of the State would be best served by processing his case through traditional criminal justice system procedures;

(16) Whether or not applicant's participation in pretrial intervention will adversely affect the prosecution of co-defendants; and

(17) Whether or not the harm done to society by abandoning criminal prosecution would outweigh the benefits to society from channeling an offender into a supervisory treatment program.

- **Reviewers:** Criminal Division Manager, County Prosecutor, and Judge

Note: The Supreme Court of New Jersey ordered the "Guidelines for Operation Of Pretrial Intervention In New Jersey," (As Amended Effective September 4, 2012) approved for implementation pursuant to R. 3:28. Guideline 3 provides additional factors that must be considered along with the criteria set forth in N.J.S.A. 2C:43-12(e).

S48.

Conditional Discharge

Conditional Discharge is a diversion program that permits the dismissal of a criminal offense by successfully completing a period of supervision (e.g. probation). In New Jersey, N.J.S.A. 2C:36A-1 establishes the Conditional Discharge program.

The New Jersey legislature created the Conditional Discharge program to service persons charged with the following DRUG or DRUG-RELATED offenses:

1.   N.J.S.A 2C:5-10(a)(4), possession of 50g or less of marijuana or 5g or less of hashish;

2.   N.J.S.A. 2C:35-10(b), using or being under the influence of CDS;

3.   N.J.S.A. 2C:35-10(c), failure to deliver CDS to police; and

4.   N.J.S.A. 2C:36-2, possession of drug paraphernalia.

In New Jersey, the Municipal Courts ordinarily handle DISORDERLY PERSONS OFFENSE matters involving DRUGS. When you successfully complete all the conditions or probationary requirements of the Conditional Discharge, the court will enter an order of dismissal, dismissing the charge(s). You can then apply for expungement six (6) months after entry of the order of dismissal according to N.J.S.A. 2C:52-6(b). See S15.

DIVERSION / SUPERVISORY TREATMENT PROGRAM

Below is a summary of the Conditional Discharge program: [3]

- **Statute:** N.J.S.A. 2C:36A-1

- **Limitations:** Disorderly persons offense or a petty disorderly persons offense involving DRUGS.

- **Eligibility:** A defendant is eligible for Conditional Discharge if he or she:

  (1) has no prior conviction for a controlled substance abuse offense, and

  (2) has never had the benefit of participation in a diversionary program.

- **Length of Probation:** between 6 to 24 months and includes random drug testing. Typically twelve (12) months. The court will usually require a drug treatment program.

- **Other:** Court has the option to suspend a defendant's driver license for 6 to 24 months.

- **Factors in Evaluating Whether the Court Should Admit an Eligible Candidate into the Conditional Discharge program:**

  (1) The nature of the offense;

  (2) The facts of the case;

  (3) The motivation and age of the defendant;

  (4) The desire of the complainant or victim to forego prosecution;

  (5) The existence of personal problems and character traits which may be related to the applicant's crime and for which services are unavailable within the criminal justice system, or which may be provided more effectively through supervisory treatment and the probability that the causes of criminal behavior can be controlled by proper treatment;

(6) The likelihood that the applicant's crime is related to a condition or situation that would be conducive to change through his participation in supervisory treatment;

(7) The needs and interests of the victim and society;

(8) The extent to which the applicant's crime constitutes part of a continuing pattern of anti-social behavior;

(9) The applicant's record of criminal and penal violations and the extent to which he may present a substantial danger to others;

(10) Whether or not the crime is of an assaultive or violent nature, whether in the criminal act itself or in the possible injurious consequences of such behavior;

(11) Consideration of whether or not prosecution would exacerbate the social problem that led to the applicant's criminal act;

(12) The history of the use of physical violence toward others;

(13) Any involvement of the applicant with organized crime;

(14) Whether or not the crime is of such a nature that the value of supervisory treatment would be outweighed by the public need for prosecution;

(15) Whether or not the applicant's involvement with other people in the crime charged or in other crime is such that the interest of the State would be best served by processing his case through traditional criminal justice system procedures;

(16) Whether or not applicant's participation in pretrial intervention will adversely affect the prosecution of co-defendants; and

(17) Whether or not the harm done to society by abandoning criminal prosecution would outweigh the benefits to society from channeling an offender into a supervisory treatment program.

S49.

Conditional Dismissal

In New Jersey, Conditional Dismissal is a diversion program that allows for an individual to avoid prosecution for petty disorderly persons offense and disorderly persons offense convictions by successfully completing a period of supervision (i.e. probation). In New Jersey, P.L. 2013, c.158, effective January 4, 2014, establishes the Conditional Dismissal program in the municipal courts.

When you successfully complete all the conditions or probationary requirements of the Conditional Dismissal, the court will enter an order of dismissal, dismissing the charge(s). After the court dismisses the charge(s) against you, you can then apply for expungement under N.J.S.A. 2C:52-6. You may have your arrest expunged six (6) months after entry of the order of dismissal according to N.J.S.A. 2C:52-6(b). See S21.

Below is a summary of the Conditional Dismissal program: [3]

- **Law:** P.L. 2013, c.158, effective January 4, 2014

- **Eligibility:** A defendant is eligible for Conditional Dismissal if he or she:

    (1) has no prior conviction for a controlled substance abuse offense;

    (2) has never had the benefit of participation in a diversionary program; and

    (3) has not been charged with organized gang activity, domestic violence as defined in the Domestic Violence Prevention Act, driving under the influence (DUI), a continuing criminal business or enterprise, a breach of the

public trust by a public officer or employee, an offense against an elderly, disabled or minor person, a violation of animal cruelty laws or a drug offense graded as a disorderly persons offense under chapter 35 or 36 of Title 2C. Drug offenses graded as disorderly persons offenses are excluded from the Conditional Dismissal program since they are eligible for diversion under the conditional discharge statute.

- **Length of Probation:** Up to twelve (12) months of monitoring.

- **Other:** Defendant must be fingerprinted as provided in N.J.S.A. 53:1-15 to allow for verification of the defendant's criminal history by the prosecutor. Person seeking admission to the conditional dismissal program must pay the court an application fee of $75. The law allows a defendant to apply for a waiver of the fee by reason of poverty.

- **Factors in Evaluating Whether the Court Should Admit an Eligible Candidate into Conditional Dismissal:**

  (1) The nature and circumstances of the offense;

  (2) The facts surrounding the commission of the offense;

  (3) The motivation, age, character, and attitude of the defendant;

  (4) The desire of the complainant or victim to forego prosecution;

  (5) The needs and interests of the victim and the community;

  (6) The extent to which the defendant's offense constitutes part of a continuing pattern of anti-social behavior;

  (7) Whether the offense is of an assaultive or violent nature, whether in the act itself or in the possible injurious consequences of such behavior;

  (8) Whether the applicant's participation will adversely affect the prosecution of co-defendants;

(9) Whether diversion of the defendant from prosecution is consistent with the public interest; and

(10) Any other factors deemed relevant by the court.

Note: Under New Jersey law, the current waiting time to expunge a disorderly persons or petty disorderly persons conviction is five (5) years. However, the recently approved Conditional Dismissal Program offers first time offenders the chance to have their record expunged six (6) months after the entry of the order of dismissal. However, only first time offenders who commit a disorderly persons or petty disorderly persons offense on or after the effective date, January 4, 2014, are eligible for the program.

S50.

Deferred Disposition / Diversion

In a "Deferred Disposition" a court adjudicates a juvenile delinquent and sets forth conditions that a juvenile must complete. If the juvenile successfully completes the terms, the court will dismiss the disposition.

Diversion is the process for removing minor juvenile cases from the court process on the condition that the juvenile completes a rehabilitative program. The juvenile must complete a Juvenile Conference Committee or a Juvenile Intake Conference. If the juvenile completes either of these programs, the court will dismiss his or her case.

CHAPTER 6:
POST-EXPUNGEMENT

S51.

Options Available If Expungement Order Is Denied

Certificate of Good Conduct / Certificate Suspending Certain Employment, Occupational Disabilities or Forfeitures

In New Jersey, a Certificate of Good Conduct (COGC) and Certificate Suspending Certain Employment, Occupational Disabilities or Forfeitures (CSCEODF) are two alternatives for a "qualified offender" to demonstrate rehabilitation in order to re-enter into the workforce. [24]; [25] The New Jersey State Parole Board (SPB) issues a COGC / CSCEODF. If the court denies your expungement order, you have the option of applying for a COGC / CSCEODF. A COGC / CSCEODF provides ex-offenders who are automatically denied a job, an occupational license, or a housing opportunity, a chance to lift the statutory limits to jobs, licensing, and housing. The effect of a COGC / CSCEODF is that a licensing authority may not automatically deny you a professional license, a job, or housing solely on the basis of your criminal conviction. [24]; [25]

The COGC / CSCEODF creates a "presumption of rehabilitation" which means that you have achieved a level of rehabilitation. However, an employer can still refuse to offer you a job or a licensing agency can still deny you a professional license if either determines that doing so would pose an unreasonable risk to property and/or others. In addition, if there is a relationship between your previous conviction and the job or license you are seeking, an employer or a licensing agency may refuse to offer you a job and/or deny you a professional license. You may obtain a COGC / CSCEODF application

POST-EXPUNGEMENT

from the SPB. (See Appendix I for statutory law on Certificate of Good Conduct and Certificate Suspending Certain Employment, Occupational Disabilities or Forfeitures.)

S52.

Must I Reveal My Prior Expunged Record From New Jersey To Another State, If Requested?

There is no authoritative answer to this question. The U.S. Constitution, Article IV, Section 1, requires that states must afford "full faith and credit" to the decision of other sister states. Title 28, Section 1738 of the United States Code enforces the "Full Faith and Credit" Clause. Although the express meaning of the "Full Faith and Credit" Clause requires a state to recognize the expungement order of a sister state and give it the same effect that it would have in the sister state, in practice it does not. Unlike New Jersey, some states require applicants to disclose prior expunged matters from a sister state. The Fifth Circuit of the United States Court of Appeals held that such practices are legal. See White v. Thomas, 660 F.2d 680, 685 (5th Cir., 1981), cert. den., 455 U.S. 1027 (1982). However, the U.S. Supreme Court has never ruled on whether a state must recognize the expungement order of its' sister state. The only legal opinion the federal courts have provided on this matter has been in the Fifth Circuit. Until the U.S. Supreme Court delivers an opinion on the issue, you should divulge your expunged New Jersey criminal record when applying for a job in a state which requires you to divulge expunged records from their sister states.

S53.

Restoring Gun Rights

Yes. Under New Jersey law, an expungement restores your gun rights. If you expunge your New Jersey criminal record, you are not required to include it in your application for a firearm in New Jersey.

The New Jersey firearms application does not require an applicant to reveal expunged convictions. Under federal law, the Lautenberg Amendment to the Violence Against Women Act prohibits firearm ownership for those convicted of domestic violence, or who are under a restraining order for domestic abuse. In addition, federal law prohibits anyone who has been convicted of a felony from owning a gun. However, if you expunge your criminal record, your firearm rights can be restored.

NOTE: The definition of domestic violence in New Jersey is more broadly defined than the federal definition of domestic violence. Therefore, a domestic violence conviction listed under the New Jersey Prevention of Domestic Violence Act may not be a domestic violence conviction listed under the federal statute.

POST-EXPUNGEMENT

The following outline summarizes the federal and New Jersey state law on firearm rights:

Federal Law - Firearm Rights

1. Any person convicted of a felony cannot legally possess or own a firearm.

2. Any person convicted of domestic violence cannot legally possess a firearm.

- The federal definition of domestic violence includes any use or attempted use of force and any use or threatened use of a deadly weapon. It includes actions related to VIOLENCE, such as homicide, assault, terroristic threats, kidnapping, criminal restraint, false imprisonment, sexual assault, and criminal sexual contact. The federal definition requires ACTUAL VIOLENCE.

- **EXCEPTION** - if your criminal record is EXPUNGED, you are eligible to restore your gun rights. Under Title 18, Section 921(a)(20)(B) of the United States Code, "What constitutes a conviction of such a crime shall be determined in accordance with the law of the jurisdiction in which the proceedings were held. Any conviction which has been expunged, or set aside or for which a person has been pardoned or has had civil rights restored shall not be considered a conviction for purposes of this chapter, unless such pardon, expungement, or restoration of civil rights expressly provides that the person may not ship, transport, possess, or receive firearms."

3. Prevents anyone who is under a restraining order for domestic abuse from owning a gun.

New Jersey - Firearm Rights

1. If your criminal record has been EXPUNGED, your firearm rights are restored, regardless of whether the conviction was for a violent crime.

POST-EXPUNGEMENT

- Domestic violence includes violence or threat of violence, abuse or harassment against a spouse, former spouse, any present or former member of the same household, someone in a dating relationship, or someone who has, or is about to have a child in common. See S.43.

- New Jersey's definition of domestic violence is broader and consists of the aforementioned acts AND acts NOT related to violence, such as lewdness, criminal mischief, burglary, criminal trespass, harassment, and stalking. In order for the federal firearm ban to apply, the offense under New Jersey's definition of domestic violence must correspond with the definition of domestic violence under federal law. Therefore, once you expunge your criminal conviction or domestic violence conviction, your gun rights will be restored. As a result, you do not have to list your expunged conviction on a firearm application.

Example 1:

Bill has a felony conviction for aggravated assault in New Jersey that has been expunged. He also has a restraining order against him for threatening to injure his ex-girlfriend. He may not have his gun rights restored because of the restraining order.

Under N.J.S.A. 2C:58-39(c)(6), "... any person who is subject to a restraining order issued pursuant to the "Prevention of Domestic Violence Act of 1991," P.L.1991, c.261 (C.2C:25-17 et seq.)...[is prohibited] from possessing any firearm."

Example 2:

Sookie has a felony conviction for possession and distribution of heroin, but it was expunged. She can have her gun rights restored because her conviction was expunged.

S54.

Immigration

Non-citizens applying for entry into the United States or seeking naturalization will likely have to divulge arrests and/or convictions, even if expunged. You cannot expunge a conviction solely for immigration purposes. The divulging of a non-citizen's arrest(s) and/or conviction(s) could result in deportation proceedings. Thus, arrest(s) and/or conviction(s), whether expunged or not, can make a person deportable or inadmissible into the United States. You should consult with a competent immigration attorney in regard to such a matter.

S55.

Jury Service

Can I serve on a jury in New Jersey if I expunge my criminal record?

Yes. In New Jersey, you may serve on a jury if you:

1. are a resident of the summoning county at the time you receive the summons;

2. are a United States citizen;

3. are physically and mentally able to perform the duties required of a juror;

4. have not pled guilty to or been convicted of an indictable offense UNLESS you have expunged your criminal record;

5. are over the age of 18; and

6. are able to read and speak English.

S56.

Can I Vote After My Petition for Expungement Is Granted?

In New Jersey, your voting rights are automatically restored after you expunge your criminal record.

S57.

Notify Private Databases

How can I update my information with private database companies?

While an expungement of your criminal record will prevent employers or the like performing an "official search" from getting access to your criminal records, it will not prevent private database companies performing an "unofficial search" from sharing your expunged record with requestors. See 1S. Therefore, you should update your information with private database companies.

The Foundation for Continuing Justice (FCJ) offers free notification service to persons who have expunged or sealed their criminal record. [9] If you have expunged your criminal record with a state and/or federal database, you will still need to notify private database/background companies of your updated record, so that it will no longer be made available to employers or the like performing an "unofficial" search. To notify private database companies of your expunged record, you must visit the FCJ at http://www.continuingjustice.org/our-projects/criminal-d atabase-update/ and "Apply for Record Clearance Update" by completing a short form. You must also attach a **certified copy** of the judge's order granting your expungement and then mail it to: [9]

Foundation For Continuing Justice
1504 Brookhollow Dr. Suite 114
Santa Ana, CA 92705

POST-EXPUNGEMENT

Generally, it takes 30 days for the FCJ to verify the authenticity of your documents and to notify the private database companies of your expunged record.

CHAPTER 8

EXPUNGEMENT SERVICES AT LEGALCLEANUP.COM

S58.

Why Choose Vonnie C. Dones III, ESQ. at www.legalcleanup.com?

We offer prospective clients in New Jersey four expungement package options ranging from the relatively low-cost Attorney Standard Package, a Do-It-Yourself attorney-reviewed package, to a full-service package involving complex cases and/or litigation. Prospective clients choose the package that best fits their budget and desired level of attorney support. Therefore, each client has complete control over the level of support he or she wishes to receive. For example, if a client wishes for our law firm to complete the expungement paperwork, but chooses to personally file the paperwork with the appropriate government offices, then we will represent the client in the specific discrete task only, and deduct and/or adjust the costs associated with such limited representation.

At Vonnie C. Dones III, ESQ., we think outside the box to provide our clients with the most practical and efficient solution to their legal needs. We are a law firm that provides legal services online. As a result, our clients do not have to pay unnecessary legal costs associated with hiring a lawyer who offers full legal representation only. Our online delivery model provides a more efficient way of servicing clients with a limited budget. What may have taken a person applying for expungement much longer to do at a much higher cost, will now take a fraction of the time at a fraction of the cost. Many law firms in the traditional sense, do not take full advantage of new technological advances that reduce the time and money associated with delivering legal services. Our online delivery model does not sacrifice or diminish the quality of workmanship, unlike unlicensed legal professionals or legal form companies who cannot provide legal advice, coaching or counseling, and can only fill-out basic forms on a person's behalf. We cut the costs associated with delivering legal services while maintaining the integrity, standards, and quality of legal services. Less time, more efficiency, equals more cash in our client's pocket. We make the process easier for our clients by simplifying document preparation. By integrating smart technology with legal advice, coaching, and document review, we provide our clients a legal solution that is user-friendly and personalized. We offer our clients a budget-conscious choice. Our online document preparation system coupled with attorney support makes the record-clearing process easier and cheaper. While our online model of delivering legal services is not entirely new to the legal profession, our added features and customized packages provide a more cost-effective, safe, and efficient way of serving those with legal needs. Again, we offer our clients the option to choose the package that fits their budget and desired level of attorney support.

In addition, we provide our clients with a secure, encrypted online client account. ClientSpace is an online client account which allows our clients to sign in their secure account and interact and/or communicate with their lawyer. [10] It is user-friendly and efficient. Our clients can get access to their ClientSpace from their computer, notebook, or tablet while sitting at home enjoying a cup of coffee. Clients are given the options of communicating via e-mail or web cam, (i.e. Skype). Clients can send and receive documents, electronically sign documents, and ask questions about their legal matter(s) at their convenience. Our online legal service is 24/7 and we respond to all messages quickly. Our clients have the advantage of having a licensed attorney by their side guiding them along the way.

S59.

Is Choosing a Legal Form Company or a so-called "Legal Professional" a bad decision?

Yes. First of all, we are comparatively cheaper than most legal form companies offering "DIY" services; and we give you, in the words of U.S. President Dwight D. Eisenhower's Secretary of Defense, Charles Erwin Wilson, "a better bang for the buck." For example, our Attorney Standard Package includes the following features: (**see prices at www.legalcleanup.com)

1. **Complete Set of Expungement Documents Ready for Filing** - We ask our clients a few questions via our online questionnaire and our automated system will assemble and generate the appropriate forms.

2. **Legal Cleanup for New Jerseyans: How To Expunge Your Criminal or Juvenile Record in New Jersey [Book]** - We provide our clients with a pdf. version of this comprehensive New Jersey Expungement Book free of charge.

3. **ClientSpace** (Online Client Account) - Our clients can complete all correspondence (communication, sending and receiving of documents, and electronic signatures) online using a secure and encrypted client account. Our client account standards meet the American Bar Association's Suggested Minimum Requirements for Law Firms Delivering Legal Services Online. Our clients have a peace of mind in knowing that all privileged information, client confidences, and data are secure and protected

as required by the American Bar and the New Jersey Bar Associations. Attorney-Client privilege applies in all correspondence as well.

4. **Removal of Expunged Records from Private Databases** - This book provides you with all the steps you will need to remove your outdated record from over 500 private databases after you have expunged your criminal record. As part of our Attorney Standard Package, we post the Foundation For Continuing Justice's (FCJ) record removal form to your ClientSpace account. After you expunge your criminal record, the appropriate court(s) and government agencies must remove your criminal record from state and federal databases. It typically takes 30-60 days to remove your expunged records from their databases. Bear in mind that private background check providers may still report your outdated record. Therefore, to make sure that private background check providers do not report your outdated record to employers or the like performing a criminal background check, it is important that you notify private database companies of your expunged or sealed record. After notification, the provider must comply with the judge's order of expungement and remove the outdated information. Generally, private database companies complete the record clearance update within thirty (30) days from the time FCJ notifies them. Other law firms or companies may charge up to $350.00 for a two-week expedited version of this private database removal service. Our clients, who purchase the Attorney Standard Package, can fill-out and mail in the removal form to the Foundation For Continuing Justice and have it processed in approximately 30 days.

> **Note:** Our law firm completes and mails the private database removal form for all clients, except for clients who purchase the Attorney Standard Package.

Secondly, document preparation companies and "legal professionals" who are not members of any State Bar are not licensed to practice law. Thus, they are not legally permitted to provide legal advice, coaching, counseling, or represent you in any legal matter. In addition, they are not held to any professional standard. Who is to say that the so-called "legal professional" can legitimately perform the legal task(s) he or she claims he or she can do? Is he or she truly qualified? A person could literally wake up one morning and say, "I think I will be a professional in law today." Why should you trust anyone to act on your behalf concerning legal matters without having any professional practice standards to abide by or any board-approved legal credentials? You should not, particularly when you can engage a licensed attorney for roughly the same costs and even better benefits.

S60.

Why Not Choose Another Law Firm?

Many law firms who offer expungement services and have an online website do not communicate or correspond with their clients or process payments from their clients through a secure web portal or client account. At Vonnie C. Dones III, ESQ., our clients can send and receive documents, sign documents electronically, access their case files 24/7, and receive legal advice, coaching, assistance and case file updates 24/7. We provide our clients with all the comforts and amenities of new and efficient web technology. Many law firms will ask potential clients to fill out a contact form or to call them for a quote or free consultation. We knock the guesswork and inconvenience out of the equation. We have a "Common Sense" policy at our law firm. "No sending a bunch of paperwork through snail mail or an unencrypted e-mail account to our clients, when we can do it securely and quickly through a protected web portal."

Many law firms or attorneys who offer expungement packages are often quoting you a price that does not include certain types of cases. Often, a law firm or an attorney may state that additional fees or extra costs may apply if: (1) you have a certain number of convictions; (2) you have a complex or litigious case; (3) you have an indictable conviction; or (4) your case is not standard. Although the price the law firm quotes you looks attractive, most of the time, it is for a basic expungement that requires very little work. Additionally, you will quickly discover that the costs associated with expungement are more than what you expected. That is why we offer prospective clients affordable and customizable expungement packages and a comprehensive list of features included in our packages.

S61.

Our Payment Plan Options

Yes. We offer flexible 2-month and 3-month payment plans for all of our expungement packages, except for our Attorney Standard Package. For more information about our payment plans, go to Pricing or Expungement Packages at www.legalcleanup.com.

S62.

24 / 7 Online Access

We notify our clients via their secure ClientSpace account in regard to any updates to their case file. We post notifications to client accounts within 24 hours of any updates or changes to their case file. Our clients may view the status of their case 24/7.

S63.

How do I Hire You as My Attorney?

First, you must visit Vonnie C. Dones III, ESQ. at www.legalcleanup.com to register for a new client account. Before we accept you as a client, you must electronically sign a limited retainer agreement or engagement letter with us stating that you agree to the terms of our limited representation. The scope of our limited representation will depend on the expungement package that you purchase. You must read the limited retainer agreement carefully. It will specify the legal services to be provided to you and define the limited scope of our representation. We offer "unbundled" legal services, as well as "bundled" legal services, but your retainer agreement with us will determine the scope of our legal representation.

Simply registering with Vonnie C. Dones III, ESQ. or signing up for a new account does not mean that you are a client of Vonnie C. Dones III, ESQ. An attorney-client relationship begins when you receive via your online account, a letter containing the limited retainer agreement signed by Vonnie C. Dones III, ESQ.

S64.

Our Money-Back Guarantee

We offer a 6-month, 100% money-back guarantee for all of our "Attorney-Reviewed Only" Documents if a court or government office rejects your application, filing, or petition due to a mistake made by the Law Firm of Vonnie C. Dones III, ESQ. (hereinafter referred to as the "Firm"). We offer a 100% money-back guarantee for our Attorney Standard and Attorney Complex Packages. We offer a 25% money-back guarantee for our Attorney Standard Pro and Attorney Complex Pro Packages if the court denies your petition or motion due to a mistake made by our law firm. The refund does not include court costs or mailing fees. The time period begins at the date of purchase. Our money-back guarantee is limited to: (1) any mistake(s) made by the Firm in filling out your legal documents or (2) any inaccurate written instructions provided to you by the Firm through your client account. To qualify for our money-back guarantee, you must provide documentation proving that the court or proper agency rejected your application, filing, or petition as a result of a mistake or inaccuracy made by the Firm. The Firm is not responsible for any incomplete or inaccurate information supplied by you to the court or proper agency. You must visit www.legalcleanup.com to apply for a full refund. You must submit a refund form, along with an official court or proper agency notice of denial, to the Firm through your secure online account.

S65.

What Expungement or Sealing Service Packages Do You Offer?

We offer the following four (4) expungement packages for our prospective clients in New Jersey:

- Attorney Standard

- Attorney Complex

- Attorney Standard Pro

- Attorney Complex Pro

Visit us at www.legalcleanup.com for package pricing.

S66.

Can You Help Me Decide Which Package is Right for Me?

If you are trying to decide which package is right for you here are some helpful points:

1.   Attorney Standard Package

- You must request your criminal history record from all appropriate government agencies involved in your case.

- You may spend approximately 8-12 hours on researching expungement law and drafting and mailing your petition and accompanying documents.

- You must make sure that your arrest(s) and/or conviction(s) are eligible for expungement. You have the option of using our online eligibility test to determine your eligibility status.

- You must make sure that you do not make any mistakes in completing and filing your expungement paperwork which may cause the court to deny your expungement without any opportunity to re-file.

- You must complete a minimum of 7 different forms. You must then mail your expungement paperwork a minimum of 15 times to a minimum of 8 different government offices without making any mistakes.

- You must personally communicate and correspond with all appropriate government agencies involved in your case.

- If the court requires you to attend a hearing, you must make a personal appearance and represent yourself in court.

2. Attorney Standard Pro Package

- We request your criminal history record from all appropriate government agencies involved in your case.

- We research the law and draft and mail your petition for expungement and accompanying paperwork.

- We make sure that you are eligible for expungement and provide a 25% money-back guarantee if we make any mistakes.

- We represent you and correspond with all government agencies on your behalf.

- We pay all the court costs and mailing fees.

- We perform a case evaluation and review all of your expungement documents to make sure that your documents are completed correctly and ready for filing.

- We prepare support evidence, if necessary for your case.

- We notify over 500+ private databases of your expunged record.

- We provide online and phone support if you have any questions or concerns.

- We provide legal advice and coaching.

3.   Attorney Complex Package

- You must request your criminal history record from all appropriate government agencies involved in your case.

- You may spend approximately 24-30 hours on researching expungement law and drafting and mailing your petition and accompanying documents.

- You must make sure that your arrest(s) and/or conviction(s) are eligible for expungement. You have the option of using our online eligibility test to determine your eligibility status.

- You must make sure that you do not make any mistakes in completing and filing your expungement paperwork which may cause your expungement application to be denied without any opportunity to re-file.

- You must complete a minimum of 10 different forms. You must then mail your expungement paperwork a minimum of 15 times to a minimum of 8 different government offices without making any mistakes. You will be required to complete ADDITIONAL PAPERWORK in a complex case. In some complex expungement matters, we do not recommend that you represent yourself.

- You will have to research statutory and case law and recent changes to the law and apply the appropriate case law to the facts of your case.

- You will have to argue your case in court in front of a judge.

- You must personally communicate and correspond with all appropriate government agencies involved in your case.

- You must respond to the prosecutor's objection in the appropriate written format.

- You will not be able to use the expungement packet from the New Jersey Judiciary.

- A hearing will be required and you must attend the hearing.

4. Attorney Complex Pro Package

- We request your criminal history record from all appropriate government agencies involved in your case.

- We research the law and draft and mail your petition for expungement and accompanying paperwork.

- We make sure that you are eligible for expungement and provide a 25% money-back guarantee if we make any mistakes.

- We represent you and correspond with all government agencies on your behalf.

- We pay all court filing and mailing fees.

- We conduct a case evaluation and review all of your expungement documents to make sure that your documents are completed correctly and ready for filing.

- We prepare support evidence, if necessary for your case.

- We notify over 500+ private databases of your expunged record.

- We provide online and phone support if you have any questions or concerns.

- We provide legal advice and coaching.

- We attend the in-court hearing and argue the case on your behalf.

- We respond in written format to the prosecutor's or a government agency's objection to your petition for expungement.

S67.

Registration Process at LegalCleanup.com

1. Why register?

You must register to create an online client account. Your account will be secure and encrypted to guarantee that all privileged information and attorney-client correspondence is kept confidential. Once registered, you may log into your account to complete the appropriate questionnaire(s) and/or document(s). As you complete the online questionnaire, you will see your document being assembled in real-time. You do not have to make a payment for your documents until you complete the Questionnaire and decide that you are ready to purchase.

2. What steps do I have to take to register?

To register for our legal services, you must go to www.legalcleanup.com and click on "Get Started." You must fill in your e-mail address in the appropriate fields and create a private username and password. You must then complete the registration process which may take a minute to complete.

3. How are expungement documents created?

If you choose to purchase our Attorney Standard or Attorney Complex Package, our automated system will generate and assemble your documents.

Our automated system will ask you a series of simple-to-follow questions and assemble your documents in real-time.

Each question includes an explanatory note and instruction to assist and guide you through completing the expungement documents correctly. A small question mark, like such " ? " by any question indicates that there is explanatory text to help you answer a question. Click on the " ? " to see the help text; click on the " ? " again to close the help text pop up box. [10]

4. Is your Web Site secure?

Through our secure, state-of-the-art hosting facilities, you will receive the highest data protection commercially available. We provide an integrated system that allows authorized parties in and keeps everyone else out through the use of: [10]

- Firewalls to prevent unauthorized access;

- SSL encryption to keep documents secure;

- U.S. government-standard 128-bit AES encryption;

- Site certificates to verify server identities;

- Secure IDs to verify user identity;

- Windows security to keep network logins locked up; and

- Intrusion protection against log-in attempt and unauthorized transmissions and off-site data storage.

5. Do you offer in-person consultations or meet with clients in your law firm office?

We are available for in-person consultations for our legal services. However, our unbundled legal services as stated in our retainer agreement, limits the scope of representation to discrete legal tasks. If you request an in-person consultation, we will be reasonably available at a mutually convenient time and place. Vonnie C. Dones III, ESQ. has no physical office in the State of

EXPUNGEMENT SERVICES BY VONNIE C. DONES III, ESQ.

New Jersey. Vonnie C. Dones III, ESQ. is located in the State of Texas. Therefore, we bill hourly for in-person consultations. Our hourly rate charges include, but are not limited to, reasonable attorney fees and travel and hotel accommodation costs. However, we do offer FREE legal consultations via e-mail, phone, and live web cam (e.g., Skype) for our clients. We recommend that you take advantage of our online technology for legal consultations.

Legal Cleanup For New Jerseyans:
Bibliography

1. John M. Cannel. NJ Criminal Code-Title 2C - Annotated. 2013 ed. Newark: Gann Law, 2013. Print.

2. New Jersey Code of Criminal Justice and Motor Vehicle Laws with Related Statutes and Court Rules. 2013 ed. New York: Thomson West, 2013. Print.

3. LexisNexis. Criminal Justice Code of New Jersey. 2013 ed. New Providence: Martindale-Hubbell, 2013. Print.

4. "New Jersey Statutes - Title 2C The New Jersey Code of Criminal Justice." - *New Jersey Attorney Resources*. N.p., n.d. Web. 24 Jan. 2014.

5. "New Jersey Statutes - Title 2C The New Jersey Code of Criminal Justice - 2C:35-10 Possession, Use or Being under the Influence, or Failure to Make Lawful Disposition."- *New Jersey Attorney Resources*. N.p., n.d. Web. 01 Feb. 2014.

6. "New Jersey Legislature." *New Jersey Legislature*. N.p., n.d. http://www.njleg.state.nj.us/. 24 Jan. 2014.

7. "Criminal Cases: PROMIS/Gavel Public Access." *Criminal Cases: PROMIS/Gavel Public Access*. N.p., n.d. Web. 24 Jan. 2014.

8. "New Jersey Courts." *New Jersey Courts*. N.p., n.d. Web. 24 Jan. 2014.

9. "Update Your Criminal Record." *Foundation For Continuing Justice*. N.p., n.d. Web. 24 Jan. 2014.

10. Granat, Richard. "DirectLaw - A Virtual Law Firm Platform Empowering Online Lawyers."*DirectLaw - A Virtual Law Firm Platform Empowering Online Lawyers*. Smart Legal Forms, Inc., 2000. Web. 24 Jan. 2014.

11. In Re Application of Fontana. 146 N.J. Super. 264. Superior Court of New Jersey, Appellate Division. 30 Dec. 1976. *Leagle*. N.p., n.d. Web. 24 Jan. 2014.

12. In Re Ross. 400 N.J. Super. 117. Superior Court of New Jersey, Appellate Division. 6 May 2008. *Leagle*. N.p., n.d. Web. 24 Jan. 2014.

13. State v. M.L. NO. A-4941-11T4. Superior Court of New Jersey, Appellate Division. 6 Feb. 2013. *Leagle*. N.p., n.d. Web. 24 Jan. 2014.

14. In Re Lobasso. 423 N.J. Super. 475, DOCKET NO. A-3577-10T4. Superior Court of New Jersey, Appellate Division. 10 Jan. 2012. Thomsom Reuters, n.d. Web. 24 Jan. 2014. http://caselaw.findlaw.com/nj-superior-court appellatedivision/1593580.html

15. State v. Zemak. 304 N.J. Super. 381. Superior Court of New Jersey, Appellate Division. 15 Apr. 1997. *Leagle*. N.p., n.d. Web. 24 Jan. 2014.

16. In Re Ronald Kollman. A-126-10. Superior Court of New Jersey, Appellate Division. 09 July 2012. *Find Law*. Thomsom Reuters, n.d. Web. 24 Jan. 2014. http://caselaw.findlaw.com/nj-supreme-court/1605623.html.

17. State v. Merendino. 293 N.J. Super. 444. Superior Court of New Jersey, Appellate Division. 27 Aug. 1996. *Leagle*. N.p., n.d. Web. 24 Jan. 2014.

18. In Re Application of R.W.B. Docket No. M-502-08. Superior Court of New Jersey, Appellate Division. 27 Aug. 1996. *Find A Case*. N.p., n.d. Web. 24 Jan. 2014.

19. In the Matter of the PETITION OF L.B. No. 88-10-0049-I. Superior Court of New Jersey, Appellate Division. 2 Feb. 2004. *New Jersey Law Journal*. N.p., n.d. Web. 24 Jan. 2014.

20. "New Jersey State Police - New Jersey Criminal History Records Checks." *New Jersey State Police - New Jersey Criminal History Records Checks*. N.p., n.d. http://www.njsp.org/about/serv_ chrc.html. 24 Jan. 2014.

21. "Federal Bureau of Investigation - Criminal History Summary Checks." Federal Bureau of Investigation - Criminal History Summary Checks. N.p., n.d. http://www.fbi.gov/about-us/cjis/criminal-history-summary checks/criminal-history-summary-checks. 24 Jan. 2014.

22. "LSNJ LAW - New Jersey's Supreme Court Provides Guidance in Filing Public Interest Expungements." Web log post. *Legal Services of New Jersey Law Website.* Legal Services of New Jersey, Nov. 2012. Web. 24 Jan. 2014.

23. "LSNJ LAW." Web log post. *Legal Services of New Jersey Law Website.* Legal Services of New Jersey, April 2010. Web. 24 Jan. 2014.

24. "New Jersey State Parole Board Documents." *New Jersey State Parole Board* |. N.p., n.d. Web. 04 Feb. 2014. <http://www.state.nj.us/parole/docs.html>.

25. "LexisNexis® Custom Solution: New Jersey Administrative Code Research Tool." LexisNexis® Custom Solution: New Jersey Administrative Code Research Tool. LexisNexis, 21 Jan. 2014. Web. 04 Feb. 2014. <http://www.lexisnexis.com/hottopics/njcode/>.

26. "Students with Criminal Convictions Have Limited Eligibility for Federal Student Aid." Students With Criminal Convictions. U.S. Department of Education, Aug. 2010. Web. 21 Feb. 2014. <http://studentaid.ed.gov/eligibility/criminal-convictions>.

27. Pilch, Tomek. "Legal and Illegal Reasons Landlords May Turn Rental Applicants Down." Nolo.com. Nolo, n.d. Web. 23 Feb. 2014. <http://www.nolo.com/legal-encyclopedia/free-books/renters-rights-book/chapter1-2.html>.

28. New Jersey Legislature "2009 New Jersey Code TITLE 2C - THE NEW JERSEY CODE OF CRIMINAL JUSTICE Section 2C:52 2C:52-27 - Effect of Expungement." Justia Law. Justia, 2009. Web. 23 Feb. 2014. <http://law.justia.com/codes/new-jersey/2009/title-2c/section-2c-52/2c-52-27>.

29. New Jersey Legislature. "2013 New Jersey Revised Statutes." Justia Law. Justia, 2013. Web. 23 Feb. 2014.<http://law.justia.com/codes/new-jersey/2013/>.

30. "New Jersey Statutes - Title 30 Institutions and Agencies - 30:4-80.8 Application for Relief." - New Jersey Attorney Resources. Onecle, 03 Sept. 2013. Web. 08 Mar. 2014. <http://law.onecle.com/new-jersey/30-institutions-and-agencies/4-80.8.html>.

31. "2009 New Jersey Code TITLE 2C - THE NEW JERSEY CODE OF CRIMINAL JUSTICE Section 2C:58 2C:58-3 - Purchase of Firearms." Justia Law. Justia US Law, n.d. Web. 08 Mar. 2014. <http://law.justia.com/codes/new-jersey/2009/title-2c/section-2c-58/2c-58-3>.

32. "New Jersey Statutes - Title 2C The New Jersey Code of Criminal Justice - 2C:43-12 Supervisory Treatment - Pretrial Intervention." - New Jersey Attorney Resources. Onecle, 03 Sept. 2013. Web. 08 Mar. 2014. <http://law.onecle.com/ new-jersey/2c-the-new-jersey-code-of-criminal-justice/43-12.html.

33. Farmer, John J. Memo, Attorney General to All County Prosecutors, All Municipal Prosecutors, State of New Jersey, Department of Law and Public Safety, Division of Criminal Justice, Trenton, N.J. Jan. 2001.

APPENDICES

APPENDIX A

New Jersey Expungement Statutes

APPENDICES

TITLE 2C. THE NEW JERSEY CODE OF CRIMINAL JUSTICE
CHAPTER 52. EXPUNGEMENT OF RECORDS

APPENDICES

2C:52-1. Definition of expungement

a. Except as otherwise provided in this chapter, expungement shall mean the extraction and isolation of all records on file within any court, detention or correctional facility, law enforcement or criminal justice agency concerning a person's detection, apprehension, arrest, detention, trial or disposition of an offense within the criminal justice system.

b. Expunged records shall include complaints, warrants, arrests, commitments, processing records, fingerprints, photographs, index cards, "rap sheets" and judicial docket records.

2C:52-2. Indictable Offenses

a. In all cases, except as herein provided, wherein a person has been convicted of a crime under the laws of this State and who has not been convicted of any prior or subsequent crime, whether within this State or any other jurisdiction, and has not been adjudged a disorderly person or petty disorderly person on more than two occasions may, after the expiration of a period of 10 years from the date of his conviction, payment of fine, satisfactory completion of probation or parole, or release from incarceration, whichever is later, present a duly verified petition as provided in section 2C:52-7 to the Superior Court in the county in which the conviction was entered praying that such conviction and all records and information pertaining thereto be expunged.

Notwithstanding the provisions of the preceding paragraph, a petition may be filed and presented, and the court may grant an expungement pursuant to this section, although less than 10 years has expired in accordance with the requirements of the preceding paragraph where the court finds:

(1) less than 10 years has expired from the satisfaction of a fine, but the 10-year time requirement is otherwise satisfied, and the court finds that the person substantially complied with any payment plan ordered pursuant to N.J.S.2C:46-1 et seq., or could not do so due to compelling circumstances affecting his ability to satisfy the fine; or

(2) at least five years has expired from the date of his conviction, payment of fine, satisfactory completion of probation or parole, or release from incarceration, whichever is later; the person has not been convicted of a crime, disorderly persons

offense, or petty disorderly persons offense since the time of the conviction; and the court finds in its discretion that expungement is in the public interest, giving due consideration to the nature of the offense, and the applicant's character and conduct since conviction. In determining whether compelling circumstances exist for the purposes of paragraph (1) of this subsection, a court may consider the amount of the fine or fines imposed, the person's age at the time of the offense, the person's financial condition and other relevant circumstances regarding the person's ability to pay.

Although subsequent convictions for no more than two disorderly or petty disorderly offenses shall not be an absolute bar to relief, the nature of those conviction or convictions and the circumstances surrounding them shall be considered by the court and may be a basis for denial of relief if they or either of them constitute a continuation of the type of unlawful activity embodied in the criminal conviction for which expungement is sought.

b. Records of conviction pursuant to statutes repealed by this Code for the crimes of murder, manslaughter, treason, anarchy, kidnapping, rape, forcible sodomy, arson, perjury, false swearing, robbery, embracery, or a conspiracy or any attempt to commit any of the foregoing, or aiding, assisting or concealing persons accused of the foregoing crimes, shall not be expunged.

Records of conviction for the following crimes specified in the New Jersey Code of Criminal Justice shall not be subject to expungement: Section 2C:11-1 et seq. (Criminal Homicide), except death by auto as specified in section 2C:11-5; section 2C:13-1 (Kidnapping); section 2C:13-6 (Luring or Enticing); section 1 of P.L.2005, c. 77 (C.2C:13-8) (Human Trafficking); section 2C:14-2 (Aggravated Sexual Assault); section 2C:14-3a (Aggravated Criminal Sexual Contact); if the victim is a minor, section 2C:14-3b (Criminal Sexual Contact); if the victim is a minor and the offender is not the parent of the victim, section 2C:13-2 (Criminal Restraint) or section 2C:13-3 (False Imprisonment); section 2C:15-1 (Robbery); section 2C:17-1 (Arson and Related Offenses); section 2C:24-4a. (Endangering the welfare of a child by engaging in sexual conduct which would impair or debauch the morals of the child); section 2C:24-4b(4) (Endangering the welfare of a child); section 2C:24-4b. (3) (Causing or permitting a child to engage in a prohibited sexual act); section 2C:24:4b.(5)(a) (Selling or manufacturing child pornography); section 2C:28-1 (Perjury); section 2C:28-2 (False Swearing); section 2C:34-1b. (4) (Knowingly promoting the prostitution of the actor's child); section 2 of P.L.2002, c. 26 (C.2C:38-2) (Terrorism); subsection a. of section 3 of P.L.2002, c. 26

APPENDICES

(C.2C:38-3) (Producing or Possessing Chemical Weapons, Biological Agents or Nuclear or Radiological Devices); and conspiracies or attempts to commit such crimes.

Records of conviction for any crime committed by a person holding any public office, position or employment, elective or appointive, under the government of this State or any agency or political subdivision thereof and any conspiracy or attempt to commit such a crime shall not be subject to expungement if the crime involved or touched such office, position or employment.

c. In the case of conviction for the sale or distribution of a controlled dangerous substance or possession thereof with intent to sell, expungement shall be denied except where the crimes relate to involve:

(1) Marijuana, where the total quantity sold, distributed or possessed with intent to sell was 25 grams or less, or;

(2) Hashish, where the total quantity sold, distributed or possessed with intent to sell was five grams or less; or

(3) Any controlled dangerous substance provided that the conviction is of the third or fourth degree, where the court finds that expungement is consistent with the public interest, giving due consideration to the nature of the offense and the petitioner's character and conduct since conviction.

d. In the case of a State licensed physician or podiatrist convicted of an offense involving drugs or alcohol or pursuant to section 14 or 15 of P.L.1989, c. 300 (C.2C:21-20 or 2C:21-4.1), the court shall notify the State Board of Medical Examiners upon receipt of a petition for expungement of the conviction and records and information pertaining thereto.

2C:52-3. Disorderly persons offenses and petty disorderly persons offenses

Any person convicted of a disorderly persons offense or petty disorderly persons offense under the laws of this State who has not been convicted of any prior or subsequent crime, whether within this State or any other jurisdiction, or of another three disorderly persons or petty disorderly persons offenses, may, after the expiration of a period of 5 years from the date of his conviction, payment of fine, satisfactory completion of probation or release from incarceration, whichever is later, present a duly verified petition as provided in section 2C:52-7 hereof to the Superior Court in the county in which the conviction was entered praying that such conviction and all records and information pertaining thereto be expunged.

2C:52-4. Ordinances

In all cases wherein a person has been found guilty of violating a municipal ordinance of any governmental entity of this State and who has not been convicted of any prior or subsequent crime, whether within this State or any other jurisdiction, and who has not been adjudged a disorderly person or petty disorderly person on more than two occasions, may, after the expiration of a period of 2 years from the date of his conviction, payment of fine, satisfactory completion of probation or release from incarceration, whichever is later, present a duly verified petition as provided in section 2C:52-7 herein to the Superior Court in the county in which the violation occurred praying that such conviction and all records and information pertaining thereto be expunged.

2C:52-4.1. Juvenile delinquent; expungement of adjudications and charges

a. Any person adjudged a juvenile delinquent may have such adjudication expunged as follows:

(1) Pursuant to N.J.S.2C:52-2, if the act committed by the juvenile would have constituted a crime if committed by an adult;

(2) Pursuant to N.J.S.2C:52-3, if the act committed by the juvenile would have constituted a disorderly or petty disorderly persons offense if committed by an adult; or

(3) Pursuant to N.J.S.2C:52-4, if the act committed by the juvenile would have constituted an ordinance violation if committed by an adult.

For purposes of expungement, any act which resulted in a juvenile being adjudged a delinquent shall be classified as if that act had been committed by an adult.

b. Additionally, any person who has been adjudged a juvenile delinquent may have his entire record of delinquency adjudications expunged if:

(1) Five years have elapsed since the final discharge of the person from legal

custody or supervision or 5 years have elapsed after the entry of any other court order not involving custody or supervision, except that periods of post-incarceration supervision pursuant to section 25 of P.L.1982, c. 77 (C.2A:4A-44), shall not be considered in calculating the five-year period for purposes of this paragraph;

(2) He has not been convicted of a crime, or a disorderly or petty disorderly persons offense, or adjudged a delinquent, or in need of supervision, during the 5 years prior to the filing the petition, and no proceeding or complaint is pending seeking such a conviction or adjudication, except that periods of post-incarceration supervision pursuant to section 25 of P.L.1982, c. 77 (C.2A:4A-44), shall not be considered in calculating the five-year period for purposes of this paragraph;

(3) He was never adjudged a juvenile delinquent on the basis of an act which if committed by an adult would constitute a crime not subject to expungement under N.J.S.2C:52-2;

(4) He has never had an adult conviction expunged; and

(5) He has never had adult criminal charges dismissed following completion of a supervisory treatment or other diversion program.

c. Any person who has been charged with an act of delinquency and against whom proceedings were dismissed may have the filing of those charges expunged pursuant to the provisions of N.J.S.2C:52-6.

2C:52-5. Expungement of records of young drug offenders

Notwithstanding the provisions of sections 2C:52-2 and 2C:52-3, after a period of not less than one year following conviction, termination of probation or parole or discharge from custody, whichever is later, any person convicted of an offense under chapters 35 or 36 of this title for the possession or use of a controlled dangerous substance, convicted of violating P.L.1955, c. 277, § 3 (C. 2A:170-77.5), [FN1] or convicted of violating P.L.1962, c. 113, § 1 (C. 2A:170-77.8), and who at the time of the offense was 21 years of age or younger, may apply to the Superior Court in the county wherein the matter was disposed of for the expungement of such person's conviction and all records pertaining thereto. The relief of expungement under this section shall be granted only if said person has not, prior to the time of hearing, violated any of the conditions of his probation or parole, albeit subsequent to discharge from probation or parole, has not been convicted of any previous or subsequent criminal act or any subsequent or previous violation of chapters 35 or 36 of this title or of P.L.1955, c. 277, § 3 (C. 2A:170-77.5) or of P.L.1962, c. 113, § 1 (C. 2A:170-77.8), or who has not had a prior or subsequent criminal matter dismissed because of acceptance into a supervisory treatment or other diversion program.

This section shall not apply to any person who has been convicted of the sale or distribution of a controlled dangerous substance or possession with the intent to sell any controlled dangerous substance except:

(1) Marihuana, where the total sold, distributed or possessed with intent to sell was 25 grams or less, or

(2) Hashish, where the total amount sold, distributed or possessed with intent to sell was 5 grams or less.

2C:52-6. Arrests not resulting in conviction

a. In all cases, except as herein provided, wherein a person has been arrested or held to answer for a crime, disorderly persons offense, petty disorderly persons offense or municipal ordinance violation under the laws of this State or of any governmental entity thereof and against whom proceedings were dismissed, or who was acquitted, or who was discharged without a conviction or finding of guilt, may at any time following the disposition of proceedings, present a duly verified petition as provided in section 2C:52-7 to the Superior Court in the county in which the disposition occurred praying that records of such arrest and all records and information pertaining thereto be expunged.

b. Any person who has had charges dismissed against him pursuant to P.L.1970, c. 226, § 27 (C. 24:21-27) or pursuant to a program of supervisory treatment, shall be barred from the relief provided in this section until 6 months after the entry of the order of dismissal.

c. Any person who has been arrested or held to answer for a crime shall be barred from the relief provided in this section where the dismissal, discharge, or acquittal resulted from a determination that the person was insane or lacked the mental capacity to commit the crime charged.

APPENDICES

2C:52-7. Petition for expungement

Every petition for expungement filed pursuant to this chapter shall be verified and include:

a. Petitioner's date of birth.

b. Petitioner's date of arrest.

c. The statute or statutes and offense or offenses for which petitioner was arrested and of which petitioner was convicted.

d. The original indictment, summons or complaint number.

e. Petitioner's date of conviction, or date of disposition of the matter if no conviction resulted.

f. The court's disposition of the matter and the punishment imposed, if any.

2C:52-8. Statements to accompany petition

There shall be attached to a petition for expungement:

a. A statement with the affidavit or verification that there are no disorderly persons, petty disorderly persons or criminal charges pending against the petitioner at the time of filing of the petition for expungement.

b. In those instances where the petitioner is seeking the expungement of a criminal conviction, a statement with affidavit or verification that he has never been granted expungement, sealing or similar relief regarding a criminal conviction by any court in this State or other state or by any Federal court. "Sealing" refers to the relief previously granted pursuant to P.L.1973, c. 191 (C. 2A:85-15 et seq.) [FN1].

c. In those instances where a person has received a dismissal of a criminal charge because of acceptance into a supervisory treatment or any other diversion program a statement with affidavit or verification setting forth the nature of the original charge, the court of disposition and date of disposition.

APPENDICES

2C:52-9. Order fixing time for hearing

Upon the filing of a petition for relief pursuant to this chapter, the court shall, by order, fix a time not less than 35 nor more than 60 days thereafter for hearing of the matter.

2C:52-10. Service of petition and documents

A copy of each petition, together with a copy of all supporting documents, shall be served pursuant to the rules of court upon the Superintendent of State Police; the Attorney General; the county prosecutor of the county wherein the court is located; the chief of police or other executive head of the police department of the municipality wherein the offense was committed; the chief law enforcement officer of any other law enforcement agency of this State which participated in the arrest of the individual; the superintendent or warden of any institution in which the petitioner was confined; and, if a disposition was made by a municipal court, upon the magistrate of that court. Service shall be made within 5 days from the date of the order setting the date for the hearing upon the matter.

2C:52-11. Order directing expungement where no objection prior to hearing

If, prior to the hearing, there is no objection from those law enforcement agencies notified or from those offices or agencies which are required to be served under 2C:52-10, and no reason, as provided in section 2C:52-14, appears to the contrary, the court may, without a hearing, grant an order directing the clerk of the court and all relevant criminal justice and law enforcement agencies to expunge records of said disposition including evidence of arrest, detention, conviction and proceedings related thereto.

2C:52-12. Denial of relief although no objection entered

In the event that none of the persons or agencies required to be noticed under 2C:52-10 has entered any objection to the relief being sought, the court may nevertheless deny the relief sought if it concludes that petitioner is not entitled to relief for the reasons provided in section 2C:52-14.

APPENDICES

2C:52-13. When hearing on petition for expungement shall not be held

No petition for relief made pursuant to this section shall be heard by any court if the petitioner, at the time of filing or date of hearing, has a charge or charges pending against him which allege the commission of a crime, disorderly persons offense or petty disorderly persons offense. Such petition shall not be heard until such times as all pending criminal and or disorderly persons charges are adjudicated to finality.

2C:52-14. Grounds for denial of relief

A petition for expungement filed pursuant to this chapter shall be denied when:

a. Any statutory prerequisite, including any provision of this chapter, is not fulfilled or there is any other statutory basis for denying relief.

b. The need for the availability of the records outweighs the desirability of having a person freed from any disabilities as otherwise provided in this chapter. An application may be denied under this subsection only following objection of a party given notice pursuant to 2C:52-10 and the burden of asserting such grounds shall be on the objector, except that in regard to expungement sought for third or fourth degree drug offenses pursuant to paragraph (3) of subsection c. of N.J.S.2C:52-2, the court shall consider whether this factor applies regardless of whether any party objects on this basis.

c. In connection with a petition under section 2C:52-6, the acquittal, discharge or dismissal of charges resulted from a plea bargaining agreement involving the conviction of other charges. This bar, however, shall not apply once the conviction is itself expunged.

d. The arrest or conviction sought to be expunged is, at the time of hearing, the subject matter of civil litigation between the petitioner or his legal representative and the State, any governmental entity thereof or any State agency and the representatives or employees of any such body.

e. A person has had a previous criminal conviction expunged regardless of the lapse of time between the prior expungement, or sealing under prior law, and the present petition. This provision shall not apply:

APPENDICES

(1) When the person is seeking the expungement of a municipal ordinance violation or,

(2) When the person is seeking the expungement of records pursuant to section 2C:52-6.

f. The person seeking the relief of expungement of a conviction for a disorderly persons, petty disorderly persons, or criminal offense has prior to or subsequent to said conviction been granted the dismissal of criminal charges following completion of a supervisory treatment or other diversion program.

2C:52-15. Records to be removed; control

If an order of expungement of records of arrest or conviction under this chapter is granted by the court, all the records specified in said order shall be removed from the files of the agencies which have been noticed of the pendency of petitioner's motion and which are, by the provisions of this chapter, entitled to notice, and shall be placed in the control of a person who has been designated by the head of each such agency which, at the time of the hearing, possesses said records. That designated person shall, except as otherwise provided in this chapter, insure that such records or the information contained therein are not released for any reason and are not utilized or referred to for

any purpose. In response to requests for information or records of the person who was arrested or convicted, all noticed officers, departments and agencies shall reply, with respect to the arrest, conviction or related proceedings which are the subject of the order, that there is no record information.

2C:52-16. Expunged record including names of persons other than petitioner

Any record or file which is maintained by a judicial or law enforcement agency, or agency in the criminal justice system, which is the subject of an order of expungement which includes the name or names of persons other than that of the petitioner need not be isolated from the general files of the agency retaining same if the other persons named in said record or file have not been granted an order of expungement of said record, provided that a copy of the record shall be given to the person designated in 2C:52-15 and the original shall remain in the agency's general files with the petitioner's name and other personal identifiers obliterated and deleted.

2C:52-17. Use of expunged records by agencies on pending petition for expungement

Expunged records may be used by the agencies that possess same to ascertain whether a person has had prior conviction expunged, or sealed under prior law, when the agency possessing the record is noticed of a pending petition for the expungement of a conviction. Any such agency may supply information to the court wherein the motion is pending and to the other parties who are entitled to notice pursuant to 2C:52-10.

2C:52-18. Supplying information to violent crimes compensation board

Information contained in expunged records may be supplied to the Violent Crimes Compensation Board, in conjunction with any claim which has been filed with said board.

2C:52-19. Order of superior court permitting inspection of records or release of information; limitations

Inspection of the files and records, or release of the information contained therein, which are the subject of an order of expungement, or sealing under prior law, may be permitted by the Superior Court upon motion for good cause shown and compelling need based on specific facts. The motion or any order granted pursuant thereto shall specify the person or persons to whom the records and information are to be shown and the purpose for which they are to be utilized. Leave to inspect shall be granted by the court only in those instances where the subject matter of the records of arrest or conviction is the object of litigation or judicial proceedings. Such records may not be inspected or utilized in any subsequent civil or criminal proceeding for the purposes of impeachment or otherwise but may be used for purposes of sentencing on a subsequent offense after guilt has been established.

2C:52-20. Use of expunged records in conjunction with supervisory treatment / diversion programs

Expunged records may be used by any judge in determining whether to grant or deny the person's application for acceptance into a supervisory treatment or diversion program for subsequent charges. Any expunged records which are possessed by any law enforcement agency may be supplied to the Attorney General, any county prosecutor or judge of this State when same are requested and are to be used for the purpose of determining whether or not to accept a person into a supervisory treatment or diversion program for subsequent charges.

2C:52-21. Use of expunged records in conjunction with setting bail, presentence report or sentencing

Expunged records, or sealed records under prior law, of prior arrests or convictions shall be provided to any judge, county prosecutor, probation department or the Attorney General when same are requested for use in conjunction with a bail hearing or for the preparation of a presentence report or for purpose of sentencing.

2C:52-22. Use of expunged records by parole board

Expunged records, or sealed records under prior law, of prior disorderly persons, petty disorderly persons and criminal convictions shall be provided to the Parole Board when same are requested for the purpose of evaluating the granting of parole to the person who is the subject of said records. Such sealed or expunged records may be used by the Parole Board in the same manner and given the same weight in its considerations as if the records had not been expunged or sealed.

2C:52-23. Use of expunged records by department of corrections

Expunged records, and records sealed under prior law, shall be provided to the Department of Corrections for its use solely in the classification, evaluation and assignment to correctional and penal institutions of persons placed in its custody.

2C:52-24. County prosecutor's obligation to ascertain propriety of petition

Notwithstanding the notice requirements provided herein, it shall be the obligation of the county prosecutor of the county wherein any petition for expungement is filed to verify the accuracy of the allegations contained in the petition for expungement and to bring to the court's attention any facts which may be a bar to, or which may make inappropriate the granting of, such relief. If no disabling, adverse or relevant information is ascertained other than that as included in the petitioner's affidavit, such facts shall be communicated by the prosecutor to the hearing judge.

APPENDICES

2C:52-25. Retroactive application

This chapter shall apply to arrests and convictions which occurred prior to, and which occur subsequent to, the effective date of this act.

2C:52-26. Vacating of orders of sealing; time; basis

If, within 5 years of the entry of an expungement order, any party to whom notice is required to be given pursuant to section 2C:52-10 notifies the court which issued the order that at the time of the petition or hearing there were criminal, disorderly persons or petty disorderly persons charges pending against the person to whom the court granted such order, which charges were not revealed to the court at the time of hearing of the original motion or that there was some other statutory disqualification, said court shall vacate the expungement order in question and reconsider the original motion in conjunction with the previously undisclosed information.

2C:52-27. Effect of expungement

Unless otherwise provided by law, if an order of expungement is granted, the arrest, conviction and any proceedings related thereto shall be deemed not to have occurred, and the petitioner may answer any questions relating to their occurrence accordingly, except as follows:

a. The fact of an expungement, sealing or similar relief shall be disclosed as provided in section 2C:52-8b.

b. The fact of an expungement of prior charges which were dismissed because of the person's acceptance into and successful completion of a supervisory treatment or other diversion program shall be disclosed by said person to any judge who is determining the propriety of accepting said person into a supervisory treatment or other diversion program for subsequent criminal charges; and

c. Information divulged on expunged records shall be revealed by a petitioner seeking employment within the judicial branch or with a law enforcement or corrections agency and such information shall continue to provide a disability as otherwise provided by law.

APPENDICES

2C:52-27.1. Practitioners convicted of health care claims fraud; rescission of debarment order

a. If an order of expungement of records of conviction under the provisions of chapter

52 of Title 2C of the New Jersey Statutes is granted by the court to a person convicted of health care claims fraud in which the court had ordered the offender's professional license be forfeited and the person be forever barred from the practice of the profession pursuant to paragraph (1) of subsection a. of section 4 of P.L.1997, c. 353 (C.2C:51-5), the person may petition the court for an order to rescind the court's order of debarment if the person can demonstrate that the person is sufficiently rehabilitated.

b. If an order to rescind the court's order of debarment is granted, the person granted the order may apply to be licensed to practice the profession from which the offender was barred.

2C:52-28. Motor vehicle offenses

Nothing contained in this chapter shall apply to arrests or conviction for motor vehicle offenses contained in Title 39.

2C:52-29. Fee

Any person who files an application pursuant to this chapter shall pay to the State Treasurer a fee of $30.00 to defer administrative costs in processing an application hereunder.

2C:52-30. Disclosure of expungement order

Except as otherwise provided in this chapter, any person who reveals to another the existence of an arrest, conviction or related legal proceeding with knowledge that the records and information pertaining thereto have been expunged or sealed is a disorderly person. Notwithstanding the provisions of section 2C:43-3, the maximum fine which can be imposed for violation of this section is $200.00.

APPENDICES

2C:52-31. Limitation

Nothing provided in this chapter shall be interpreted to permit the expungement of records contained in the Controlled Dangerous Substances Registry created pursuant to P.L.1970, c. 227 (C. 26:2G-17 et seq.), [FN1] or the registry created by the Administrative Office of the Courts pursuant to section 2C:43-21.

2C:52-32. Construction

This chapter shall be construed with the primary objective of providing relief to the one-time offender who has led a life of rectitude and disassociated himself with unlawful activity, but not to create a system whereby periodic violators of the law or those who associate themselves with criminal activity have a regular means of expunging their police and criminal records.

APPENDIX B

New Jersey County Courthouse Directory

The following is a list of the New Jersey Criminal Case Management Offices by county. We recommend that you verify the addresses and contact numbers. You can find an updated directory by visiting the New Jersey Courts website at http://www.judiciary.state.nj.us/

APPENDICES

New Jersey Superior Court Criminal Case Management Offices by County
All Counties: Filing fee: $52.50 Payee: State of N.J. Treasurer

Atlantic County
Sup Crt. of Atlantic Co.
Expungement Clerk
4997 Unami Boulevard
Mays Landing, NJ 08330
(609) 625-7000 / (609) 909-8147

Bergen County
Case Management Office
Bergen County Justice Center
10 Main Street, Room 119
Hackensack, NJ 07601
(201) 527-2400 / (201) 795-6701

Burlington County
Burlington County Courthouse
Processing Office
49 Rancocas Road, 1st floor
Mount Holly, NJ 08060
(609) 518-2573

Camden County
Hall of Justice
Expungement Section
101 South Fifth Street
Camden, NJ 08103
(856) 379-2200 ext. 3364

Cape May County
Criminal Case Management
9 N. Main Street
Cape May Court House, NJ 08210
(609) 463-6550

Cumberland County
Criminal Case Manager
P.O. Box 757
Bridgeton, NJ 08302
(609) 453-4300

Essex County
Veterans Courthouse
Criminal Records Office
50 West Market Street
Room 1012
Newark, NJ 07102
(973) 693-6863

Hudson County
Criminal Records
Criminal Case Management
Administration Bldg.
595 Newark Ave., Rm. 104
Jersey City, NJ 07306
(201) 217-5217

Hunterdon County
Criminal Division
Hunterdon Justice Center
65 Park Avenue
Flemington, NJ 08822
(908) 237-5840

Gloucester County
Criminal Case Manager
Hunter and Euclid Streets
Woodbury, NJ 08096
(856) 853-3200

Mercer County
Mercer County Superior Court
Criminal Records Exp. Unit
209 South Broad St., Room 200
Trenton, NJ 08650
(609) 571-4127

Middlesex County
Middlesex County Court House
Criminal Records
56 Paterson Street
P.O. Box 964
New Brunswick, NJ 08903-0964
(732) 519-3859

Monmouth County
Monmouth County Superior Crt.
Criminal Division
P.O. Box 1271
Freehold, NJ 07728
(732) 677-4500

Morris County
Superior Court of New Jersey
Criminal Records Department
P.O. Box 910
Morristown, NJ 07963
(973) 326-6950

Ocean County
Ocean County Superior Court
Criminal Case Processing
120 Hooper Avenue
Toms River, NJ 08753
(732) 929-4780

Passaic County
Superior Court
Criminal Division
77 Hamilton Street, 2nd Floor
Paterson, NJ 07505
(973) 247-8402

Salem County
Criminal Case Management
92 Market Street
P.O. Box 78
Salem, NJ 08079
(609) 935-7510, Ext. 8279

Somerset County
20 North Bridge Street
P.O. Box 3000
Somerville, NJ 08876
(908) 231-7600 Ext. 762

Sussex County
Sussex County Judicial Center
Criminal Division
43-47 High Street
Newton, NJ 07860
(973) 579-0933

Union County
Criminal Division
2 Broad Street
Elizabeth, NJ 07207
(908) 659-4660

Warren County
Criminal Case Management
P.O. Box 900
Belvidere, NJ 07823
(908) 475-6990

APPENDIX C

New Jersey County Prosecutor Offices Directory

The following is a list of the New Jersey Prosecutor Offices by county. We recommend that you verify the addresses and contact numbers. You can find an updated directory by visiting the New Jersey Courts website at http://www.judiciary.state.nj.us/

APPENDICES

New Jersey County Prosecutor Offices by County

Atlantic County
4997 Unami Blvd
PO Box 2002
Mays Landing, NJ 08330
Phone: (609) 909-7800
Fax: (609) 909-7802

Bergen County
Justice Center
10 Main St.
Hackensack, NJ 07601-7681
Phone: (201) 646-2300
Fax: (201) 646-3794

Burlington County
County Courts Facility
49 Rancocas Rd.
PO Box 6000
Mount Holly, NJ 08060
Phone: (609) 265-5035

Camden County
25 North 5th St.
Camden, NJ 08102-1231
Phone: (856) 225-8400
Fax: (856) 963-0080
Phone: (609) 465-1135
Fax: (609) 465-1347

Cape May County
Crest Haven Complex
4 Moore Rd.
110 Justice Way
Cape May Court House, NJ 08210

Cumberland County
43 Fayette St.
Bridgeton, NJ 08302
Phone: (856) 453-0486
Fax: (856) 451-1507

Essex County
Veterans Courthouse
50 West Market St
Newark, NJ 07102
Phone: (973) 621-4700
Fax: (973) 621-4560

Gloucester County
PO Box 623
Woodbury, NJ 08096
Phone: (856) 384-5500
Fax: (856) 384-8624

Hudson County
Administration Building
595 Newark Ave, 6th Fl.
Jersey City, NJ 07306
Phone: (201) 795-6400
Fax: (201) 795-3365

Hunterdon County
Justice Center
65 Park Ave.
PO Box 756
Flemington, NJ 08822-0756
Phone: (908) 788-1129
Fax: (908) 806-4618

Mercer County
County Court House
209 South Broad St, 3rd Fl.
PO Box 8068
Trenton, NJ 08650
Phone: (609) 989-6350
Fax: (609) 989-0161

Middlesex County
25 Kirkpatrick St, 3rd Fl.
New Brunswick, NJ 08901
Phone: (732) 745-3300
Fax: (732) 745-2791

Monmouth County
132 Jerseyville Ave
Freehold, NJ 07728
Phone: (732) 431-7160
Fax: (732) 409-3673

Morris County
Administration & Records Building
PO Box 900
Morristown, NJ 07963-0900
Phone: (973) 285-6200
Fax: (973) 285-6226

Ocean County
119 Hooper Ave.
PO Box 2191
Toms River, NJ 08754
Phone: (732) 929-2027
Fax: (732) 506-5088

Passaic County
Administration Building
401 Grand St.
Paterson, NJ 07505
Phone: (973) 881-4800

Salem County
87 Market St.
PO Box 462
Salem, NJ 08079
Phone: (856) 935-7510 Ext. 8333
Fax: (856) 935-8737

Somerset County
40 North Bridge St.
P.O. Box 3000
Somerville, NJ 08876
Phone: (908) 231-7100
Fax: (908) 704-0056

Sussex County
19-21 High St.
Newton, NJ 07860
Phone: (973) 383-1570
Fax: (973) 383-4929

Union County
32 Rahway Ave.
Elizabeth, NJ 07202-2115
Phone: (908) 527-4500
Fax: (908) 289-1267

Warren County
Court House
413 Second St.
Belvidere, NJ 07823
Phone: (908) 475-6275

APPENDIX D

New Jersey County Identification Bureaus Directory

The following is a list of the New Jersey County Identification Bureaus. We recommend that you verify the addresses and contact numbers. You can find an updated directory by visiting the New Jersey Courts website at http://www.judiciary.state.nj.us/

APPENDICES

New Jersey County Identification Bureaus

Atlantic County
Atlantic County Sheriff
4997 Unami Blvd.
Mays Landing, NJ 08330
Attention: I.D. Bureau

Bergen County
Bureau of Criminal Identification
Bergen County Sheriff
160 South River Street
Hackensack, NJ 07601

Burlington County
Burlington County Sheriff
49 Rancocas Road
Mount Holly, NJ 08060
Attention: Expungement

Camden County
Camden County Sheriff
P.O. Box 769
Camden, NJ 08101
Attention: I. D. Bureau

Cape May County
Cape May County Sheriff
4 Moore Road
Cape May Court House
NJ, 08210
Attention: I.D. Bureau

Cumberland County
Cumberland County Sheriff
220 N. Laurel Street
Bridgeton, NJ 08302
Attention: I.D. Bureau

Essex County
Essex County Sheriff–B.C.I.
New Courts Building
2nd Floor, 50 Nelson Place
Newark, NJ 07102

Gloucester County
Gloucester County Sheriff
Criminal Justice Complex
P.O. Box 376
Woodbury, NJ 08096

Hudson County
Hudson County Sheriff
Attention: B.C.I.
Administrative Building
595 Newark Avenue
Jersey City, NJ 07306

Hunterdon County
Hunterdon County Sheriff
P.O. Box 2900
Flemington, NJ 08822
Attention: I.D. Bureau

Mercer County
Mercer County Sheriff
P.O. Box 8068
Trenton, NJ 08650

Middlesex County
Middlesex County Sheriff
701 Livingston Avenue
New Brunswick, NJ 08901
Attention: Records

Monmouth County
Monmouth County
Criminal Identification Bureau
50 E. Main Street
Freehold, NJ 07728

Morris County
Morris County Sheriff
P.O. Box 900
Morristown, NJ 07963-900
Attention: C.I.D.

Ocean County
Ocean County Sheriff
120 Hooper Avenue
Toms River, NJ 08753
Attention: I.D. Bureau

Passaic County
Passaic County Sheriff
Criminal Identification Bureau
11 Sheriff's Plaza
Paterson, NJ 07501

Salem County
Salem County Sheriff
Identification Bureau
94 Market Street
Salem, NJ 08079

Somerset County
Somerset County Sheriff
P.O. Box 3000
Somerville, NJ 08876
Attention: I.D. Bureau

Sussex County
Sussex County Sheriff
39 High Street
Newton, NJ 07860
Attention: Records

Union County
Union County Sheriff
10 Elizabethtown Plaza
Elizabeth, NJ 07207
Attention: I.D. Bureau

Warren County
Warren County Sheriff
413 Second Street
Courthouse
Belvidere, NJ 07823
Attention: Warrant Officer

APPENDIX E

New Jersey Superior Court Family Division Offices Directory

The following is a list of the New Jersey Superior Court Family Division Offices. We recommend that you verify the addresses and contact numbers. You can find an updated directory or contact list by visiting the New Jersey Courts website at http://www.judiciary.state.nj.us/

APPENDICES

New Jersey Superior Court Family Division Offices

Atlantic County
Atlantic County Civil Courthouse
Family Division, Direct Filing
1201 Bacharach Blvd., West Wing
Atlantic City, NJ 08401
(609)-345-6700

Bergen County
Justice Ctr, Room 119
10 Main Street
Hackensack, NJ 07601
(201)-527-2300

Burlington County
Burlington Cty Ctrl Processing OFC
Attention: Dissolution Intake
Courts Facility, 1st Floor
49 Rancocas Road
Mount Holly, NJ 08060
(609)-518-2621

Camden County
Camden County Family Division
Hall of Justice 2nd Floor
101 S. 5th Street
Camden, NJ 08103-4001
(856) 379-2204

Cape May County
Superior Crt Chancery, Fam. Div.
4 Moore Road
Cape May Courthouse, NJ 08210
(609)-463-6600

Cumberland County
Cumberland County Family Division
60 W. Broad St.
Bridgeton, NJ 08302
856-453-4564

Essex County
Family Division Dissolution Unit
Wilentz Justice Complex, Rm 113
212 Washington Street
Newark, NJ 07102
(973)-693-6710

Family Div. Non-Dissolution Unit
Wilentz Justice Complex, Rm 1365
212 Washington Street
Newark, NJ 07012
(973)-693-5560 or (973)-693-5520

Gloucester County
Family Division
Gloucester Cty Justice Complex
70 Hunter Street
Woodbury, NJ 08096
(856)-686-7400

Hudson County
Family Intake Team
Administration Bldg., Room 203
595 Newark Avenue
Jersey City, NJ 07306
(201)-795-5668

Hunterdon County
Family Case Management Office
Hunterdon County Justice Center
65 Park Avenue
Flemington, NJ 08822

Mercer County
Family Case Management Office
175 S. Broad St., 2nd Floor
P.O. Box 8068
Trenton, NJ 08650-0068
(609) -571-4200

Middlesex County
Family Part Intake Reception Team
Family Courthouse
120 New St.
P.O. Box 2691
New Brunswick, NJ 08903-2691
(732)-981-3008

Monmouth County
Family Part, Courthouse
71 Monument Park
P.O. Box 1252
Freehold, NJ 07728-1252
(732)-677-4050

Morris County
Morris County Family Division
Morris Cty Crthouse Fam. Intake
Washington and Court Streets
P.O. Box 910
Morristown, NJ 07963
973-656-4346

Ocean County
Ocean County Dissolution Unit
214 Justice Complex
120 Hooper Avenue
Toms River, NJ 08754
(732)-929-2033

Passaic County
Passaic County Superior Court
Family Division
Cty Administration Bldg. 8th Floor
401 Grand Street
Paterson, NJ 07505
(973)-247-8459

Salem County
Family Court Intake Courthouse
92 Market St.
P.O. Box 223
Salem, NJ 08079
(856)-935-7510

Somerset County
Family Case Management Office
Courthouse, 2nd Floor
P.O. Box 3000
Somerville, NJ 08876-1262
(908)-231-7600

APPENDICES

Sussex County
Sussex County Family Division
Sussex County Judicial Center
43-47 High Street
Newton, NJ 07860
(973)-579-0630

Union County
Dissolution Assignment Office
New Annex Bldg.; Courthouse
2 Broad Street
Elizabeth, NJ 07207
(908)-659-3314

Warren County
Family Division Dissolution Unit
Courthouse
413 Second St.
P.O. Box 900
Belvidere, NJ 07823-1500
(908)-475-6150

APPENDIX F

New Jersey Probation Division Offices Directory

The following is a list of the New Jersey Probation Division Offices. We recommend that you verify the addresses and contact numbers. You can find an updated directory or contact list by visiting the New Jersey Courts website at http://www.judiciary.state.nj.us/

APPENDICES

New Jersey Probation Division Offices

Atlantic County
Vicinage Chief Probation Officer
Atlantic County Probation Division
1201 Bacharach Blvd
PO Box 5129
Atlantic City, NJ 08404

Bergen County
Vicinage Chief Probation Officer
Bergen County Probation Division
133 River St
Hackensack, NJ 07601

Burlington County
Vicinage Chief Probation Officer
Burlington Cty Probation Division
50 Rancocas Rd
PO Box 6555
Mt. Holly, NJ 08060

Camden County
Vicinage Chief Probation Officer
Camden County Probation Div
6 Exec Campus, Ste 300, Rte 70
PO Box 8107
Cherry Hill, NJ 08002

Cape May County
Vicinage Chief Probation Officer
Cape May County Probation Div
Courthouse
9 Main St
Cape May Courthouse, NJ 08210

Cumberland County
Vicinage Chief Probation Officer
Cumberland Cty Probation Division
Court House
PO Box 636
Bridgeton, NJ 08302

Essex County
Vicinage Chief Probation Officer
Essex County Probation Division
60 Evergreen Pl, 8th Fl
East Orange, NJ 07018

Gloucester County
Vicinage Chief Probation Officer
Gloucester County Probation Div
PO Box 638
Woodbury, NJ 08096

Hudson County
Vicinage Chief Probation Officer
Hudson County Probation Division
595 Newark Ave, Rm 406
Jersey City, NJ 07306

Hunterdon County
Vicinage Chief Probation Officer
Hunterdon County Probation Div
65 Park Ave
Flemington, NJ 08822

Mercer County
Vicinage Chief Probation Officer
Mercer County Probation Division
175 South Broad St
PO Box 8068
Trenton, NJ 08650-0068

Middlesex County
Vicinage Chief Probation Officer
Middlesex County Probation Div
1 JFK Sq
Administration Bldg.
P.O. Box 789
New Brunswick, NJ 08903

Monmouth County
Vicinage Chief Probation Officer
Monmouth County Probation Div
2407 Rte 66
Ocean, NJ 07712

Morris County
Vicinage Chief Probation Officer
Morris County Probation Division
Courthouse
PO Box 910
Morristown, NJ 07963-0910

Ocean County
Vicinage Chief Probation Officer
Ocean County Probation Division
120 Hooper Ave
Toms River, NJ 08754

Passaic County
Vicinage Chief Probation Officer
Passaic County Probation Division
63-65 Hamilton St
Paterson, NJ 07505

Salem County
Vicinage Chief Probation Officer
Salem County Probation Division
85 Market St
Salem, NJ 08079

Somerset County
Vicinage Chief Probation Officer
Somerset County Probation Div
North Bridge & Main St
PO Box 3000
Somerville, NJ 08876-1262

Sussex County
Vicinage Chief Probation Officer
Sussex County Probation Division
43-47 High St
Newton, NJ 07860

Union County
Vicinage Chief Probation Officer
Union County Probation Division
1143-45 East Jersey St
Elizabeth, NJ 07207

Warren County
Vicinage Chief Probation Officer
Warren County Probation Division
413 2nd St
PO Box 900
Belvidere, NJ 07823-1500

APPENDIX G

Federal Bureau of Investigation Criminal History Summary Request Process

APPENDICES

The following information was taken directly from the Federal Bureau of Investigation website at http://www.fbi.gov/about-us/cjis/criminal-history-sum mary-checks/criminal-history-summary-checks. [21]

The Federal Bureau of Investigation (FBI) reports on their website the following two options for requesting your Criminal History Summary or proof that it does not exist:

Option 1: Submit your request directly to the FBI.

> **Step 1**: Complete the Applicant Information Form.
>
> - If the request is for a couple, family, etc., all persons must sign the form. Include your complete mailing address. Please provide your telephone number and/or e-mail address, if available.

Note: Effective October 12, 2013, the FBI no longer accepts return self-addressed stamped envelopes with Departmental Order request.

> **Step 2**: Obtain a set of your fingerprints.
>
> - Provide the original fingerprint card. Previously processed cards or copies will not be accepted.
>
> - Your name and date of birth must be provided on the fingerprint card. Fingerprints should be placed on a standard fingerprint form (FD-258) commonly used for applicant or law enforcement purposes.
>
> - Include rolled impressions of all 10 fingerprints and impressions of all 10 fingerprints take simultaneously (these are sometimes referred to as plain or flat impressions).
>
> - If possible, have your fingerprints taken by a fingerprinting technician. This service may be available at a law enforcement agency.
>
> - Fingerprints taken with ink or via live scan are acceptable.

- To ensure the most legible prints possible, refer to the Recording Legible Fingerprints brochure. If fingerprints are not legible, the fingerprint card will be rejected. This could cause delays in processing and could also result in additional fees.

Step 3: Submit payment.

- Option 1: Pay by credit card using the Credit Card Payment Form. Don't forget to include the expiration date of the credit card that you are using.

- Option 2: Obtain a money order or certified check for $18 U.S. dollars made payable to the Treasury of the United States. Please be sure to sign where required.

- Important note: Cash, personal checks, or business checks WILL NOT be accepted and sending any of these will delay processing of your request.

- Payment must be for the exact amount.

- If the request is for a couple, family, etc., include $18 for each person.

Step 4: Review the Criminal History Summary Request Checklist to ensure that you have included everything you need to process your request.

Step 5: Mail the required items listed above—signed applicant information form, fingerprint card, and payment of $18 U.S. dollars for each person or copy requested—to the following address:

FBI CJIS Division– Summary Request
1000 Custer Hollow Road
Clarksburg, WV 26306

Note: Although the FBI employs the most efficient methods for processing these requests, processing times may take approximately five to six weeks depending on the volume of requests received. For assistance, contact the Customer Service Group at (304) 625-5590

Option 2: Submit to an FBI-approved Channeler, which is a private business that has contracted with the FBI to receive the fingerprint submission and relevant data, collect the associated fee(s), electronically forward the fingerprint submission with the necessary information to the FBI CJIS Division for a national Criminal History Summary check, and receive the electronic summary check result for dissemination to the individual. Contact each Channeler for processing times. FBI-approved Channelers receive the fingerprint submission and relevant data, collect the associated fee(s), electronically forward the fingerprint submission with the necessary information to the FBI CJIS Division for a national Criminal History Summary check, and receive the electronic summary check result for dissemination to the individual. An FBI-approved Channeler simply helps expedite the delivery of Criminal History Summary information on behalf of the FBI.

The process for making a request through an FBI-approved Channeler is consistent with FBI submission procedures. Please note that an FBI-approved Channeler may have different methods or processes for submissions. Furthermore, additional fees may apply above the FBI fee for requests submitted through an FBI-approved Channeler. Contact each Channeler for processing times.

An individual requesting a Criminal History Summary or proof that a summary does not exist through FBI-approved Channelers should contact the Channeler directly for complete information and instructions.

Note: Please review the information below regarding the use of FBI-approved Channelers:

- An FBI-approved Channeler may only process requests for a U.S. person (an individual who is a citizen of the U.S. or a lawful permanent resident of the U.S.). A lawful permanent resident is any person not a citizen of the U.S. who is residing in the U.S. under legally recognized and lawfully recorded permanent residence as an immigrant (also known "Permanent Resident Alien," "Resident Alien Permit Holder," and "Green Card Holder").

- If an authentication (apostille) is needed, contact the Channeler to determine if this service is provided.

APPENDICES

- An FBI-approved Channeler cannot process a request for employment and/or licensing purposes within the United States.

- This type of request should be coordinated with the appropriate state identification bureau (or state police) for the correct procedures."

List of FBI-Approved Channelers for Departmental Order Submissions

3M Cogent Systems
www.cogentid.com
(614) 718-9691

Accurate Biometrics
www.accuratebiometrics.com
(773) 685-5699

Daon Trusted Identity Services, Inc.
Services, Inc.
www.DaonTIS.com
(703) 797-2550

Eid Passport, Inc.
www.eidpassport.com
(855) 531-5827

Fieldprint, Inc.
www.fieldprint.com/FBI
(877) 614-4364

Inquiries, Inc.
www.inquiriesinc.com
(866) 987-3767

IBT, LLC by MorphoTrust
www.IdentoGO.com/FBICheck
(877) 783-4187

National Background Check, Inc.
www.nationalbackgroundcheck.com
(877) 932-2435

National Credit Reporting
www.myFBIreport.com
(800) 441-1661

TRP Associates, LLC dba ID Solutions
www.trpassociates.net
(401) 736-4300

VetConnex
www.vetconnex.com
(952) 224-8656

APPENDIX H

Adoption, Child Placement, & Investigation Statute

APPENDICES

TITLE 30. INSTITUTIONS AND AGENCIES
Chapter 4C. PLACING CHILD IN RESOURCE FAMILY HOME OR INSTITUTION

30:4C-26.8 Adoptive, resource family parent, investigation.

1. a. A person, in addition to meeting other requirements as may be established by the Department of Children and Families, shall become a resource family parent or eligible to adopt a child only upon the completion of an investigation to ascertain if there is a State or federal record of criminal history for the prospective adoptive or resource family parent or any other adult residing in the prospective parent's home. The investigation shall be conducted by the Division of State Police in the Department of Law and Public Safety and shall include an examination of its own files and the obtaining of a similar examination by federal authorities.

b. If the prospective resource family parent or any adult residing in the prospective parent's home has a record of criminal history, the Department of Children and Families shall review the record with respect to the type and date of the criminal offense and make a determination as to the suitability of the person to become a resource family parent or the suitability of placing a child in that person's home, as the case may be.

c. For the purposes of this section, a conviction for one of the offenses enumerated in subsection d. or e. of this section has occurred if the person has been convicted under the laws of this State or any other state or jurisdiction for an offense that is substantially equivalent to the offenses enumerated in these subsections.

d. A person shall be disqualified from being a resource family parent or shall not be eligible to adopt a child if that person or any adult residing in that person's household ever committed a crime which resulted in a conviction for:

(1) a crime against a child, including endangering the welfare of a child and child pornography pursuant to N.J.S.2C:24-4; or child abuse, neglect, or abandonment pursuant to R.S.9:6-3;

(2) murder pursuant to N.J.S.2C:11-3 or manslaughter pursuant to N.J.S.2C:11-4;

(3) aggravated assault which would constitute a crime of the second or third degree pursuant to subsection b. of N.J.S.2C:12-1;

(4) stalking pursuant to P.L.1992, c.209 (C.2C:12-10);

(5) kidnapping and related offenses including criminal restraint; false imprisonment; interference with custody; criminal coercion; or enticing a child into a motor vehicle, structure, or isolated area pursuant to N.J.S.2C:13-1 through 2C:13-6;

(6) sexual assault, criminal sexual contact, or lewdness pursuant to N.J.S.2C:14-2 through N.J.S.2C:14-4;

(7) robbery which would constitute a crime of the first degree pursuant to N.J.S.2C:15-1;

(8) burglary which would constitute a crime of the second degree pursuant to N.J.S.2C:18-2;

(9) domestic violence pursuant to P.L.1991, c.261 (C.2C:25-17 et seq.);

(10) endangering the welfare of an incompetent person pursuant to N.J.S.2C:24-7 or endangering the welfare of an elderly or disabled person pursuant to N.J.S.2C:24-8;

(11) terrorist threats pursuant to N.J.S.2C:12-3;

(12) arson pursuant to N.J.S.2C:17-1, or causing or risking widespread injury or damage which would constitute a crime of the second degree pursuant to N.J.S.2C:17-2; or

(13) an attempt or conspiracy to commit an offense listed in paragraphs (1) through (12) of this subsection.

e. A person shall be disqualified from being a resource family parent if that person or any adult residing in that person's household was convicted of one of the following crimes and the date of release from confinement occurred during the preceding five years:

(1) simple assault pursuant to subsection a. of N.J.S.2C:12-1;

(2) aggravated assault which would constitute a crime of the fourth degree pursuant to subsection b. of N.J.S.2C:12-1;

(3) a drug-related crime pursuant to P.L.1987, c.106 (C.2C:35-1 et seq.);

(4) robbery which would constitute a crime of the second degree pursuant to N.J.S.2C:15-1;

(5) burglary which would constitute a crime of the third degree pursuant to N.J.S.2C:18-2; or

(6) an attempt or conspiracy to commit an offense listed in paragraphs (1) through (5) of this subsection.

For the purposes of this subsection, the "date of release from confinement" means the date of termination of court-ordered supervision through probation, parole, or residence in a correctional facility, whichever date occurs last.

For purposes of this section, "resource family parent" means any person with whom a child in the care, custody, or guardianship of the Department of Children and Families is placed by the department, or with its approval, for care and shall include any person with whom a child is placed by the Division of Child Protection and Permanency for the purpose of adoption until the adoption is finalized.

APPENDIX I

Certificate of Good Conduct and Certificate Suspending Certain Employment, Occupational Disabilities or Forfeitures Statutes

APPENDICES

In New Jersey, the New Jersey Administrative Code governs the following statutory laws that apply to Certificates of Good Conduct and Certificates Suspending Certain Employment, Occupational Disabilities or Forfeitures:

Certificate of Good Conduct

TITLE 10A. CORRECTIONS
CHAPTER 71. PAROLE
SUBCHAPTER 8. CERTIFICATE OF GOOD CONDUCT

§ 10A:70-8.1 Definition of certificate of good conduct

(a) The Certificate of Good Conduct is a document issued by the board to assist the rehabilitation of convicted offenders by removing impediments and restrictions upon their ability to obtain a proposed employment.

(b) The Certificate of Good Standing does not imply pardon and under no circumstances is it to be construed as forgiving, absolving or mitigating the offense(s).

(c) Issuance of a Certificate of Good Conduct pursuant to N.J.S.A. 2A:168A-1 et seq. precludes a licensing authority, as defined in N.J.S.A. 2A:168A-2, from disqualifying or discriminating against the applicant because of any conviction for a crime, unless N.J.S.A. 2A:93-5 is applicable.

§ 10A:70-8.2. Eligibility

(a) An application for a Certificate of Good Conduct shall not be entertained unless the applicant meets all of the following requirements:

1. The applicant was previously paroled by the Board;

2. At least two years have passed since the date any similar application was denied, unless the board determines that significant information exists which provides a basis for a waiver of this limitation.

APPENDICES

§ 10A:70-8.3. Procedure

(a) The applicant shall apply to the Board for a Certificate of Good Conduct on forms prescribed and furnished by the Board.

(b) Upon receipt of the application, the Board shall initiate a confidential investigation which shall indicate all pertinent legal and social information, with particular reference to the need the applicant has and the use he or she expects to make to the certificate.

(c) The applicant shall be required to furnish all documentary evidence the Board shall require, except as herein provided.

(d) The applicant shall have the right to restrict the Board's investigation. In such a case, the Board's investigator shall note in his or her report the limitations placed on the inquiry by the applicant, and the Board shall evaluate such limitations when considering the application.

§ 10A:70-8.4. Criteria

The Board shall evaluate the application on the basis of the applicant having achieved a degree of rehabilitation indicating that his or her engaging in the proposed employment would not be incompatible with the welfare of society.

§ 10A:70-8.5. Notification

(a) The Board shall notify the applicant of its decision within 30 days of the date the application was considered.

(b) A copy of the Certificate of Good Conduct, if granted, shall be filed with the Secretary of State.

§ 10A:71-8.6 Revocation of Certificate of Good Conduct

The Board may revoke a Certificate of Good Conduct for good cause.

APPENDICES

§ 10A:70-8.7. Board action

The Board shall grant a revoke of Certificate of Good Conduct by majority vote of its members.

NOTE: 2A:167-5.

Any person who has been convicted of a crime and by reason thereof has been deprived of the right of suffrage or of any other of his civil rights or privileges, or upon whom there has been imposed a fine or who has suffered a forfeiture, except disqualification to hold and enjoy any public office of honor, profit or trust in this state under judgment of impeachment, may make application for the restoration of the right of suffrage or of such other rights or privileges or for the suspension or remission of such fine or forfeiture, which application the governor may grant by order signed by him.

Certificate Suspending Certain Employment, Occupational Disabilities or Forfeitures

TITLE 10A. CORRECTIONS
CHAPTER 71. PAROLE
SUBCHAPTER 9. CERTIFICATE SUSPENDING CERTAIN EMPLOYMENT, OCCUPATIONAL DISABILITIES OR FORFEITURES

§ 10A:71-9.1 Authorization to issue certificate

(a) A certificate may be issued by the Board in the case of a person who was under parole supervision in accordance with the provisions of N.J.S.A. 2A:168A-7, which suspends certain disabilities, forfeitures or bars to employment or professional licensure or certification that apply to persons convicted of criminal offenses.

(b) A certificate issued by the Board pursuant to N.J.S.A. 2A:168A-7 shall have the effect of relieving disabilities, forfeitures or bars, except those established or required by Federal law, to:

    1. Public employment;

2. Qualification for a license or certification to engage in the practice of a profession, occupation or business, except the practice of law; or

3. Admission to an examination to qualify for such a license or certification, except for the bar examination, or an examination for a law enforcement, homeland security, or emergency management position. (c) A certificate issued by the Board pursuant to N.J.S.A. 2A:168A-7 may be limited to one or more enumerated disabilities, forfeitures or bars, or may relieve the subject of all disabilities, forfeitures or bars that may be affected by N.J.S.A. 2A:168A-7.

§ 10A:71-9.2 Definitions

The following words or terms, as used in this subchapter, shall have the following meanings, unless the context clearly indicates otherwise:

"Public employment" shall mean employment by a State, county, or municipal agency, but shall not include elected office, or employment in law enforcement, corrections, the judiciary, in a position related to homeland security or emergency management, or any position that has access to sensitive information that could threaten the public health, welfare, or safety.

"Qualified offender" refers to a person who has one criminal conviction or who has convictions for more than one crime charged in separate counts of one indictment or accusation. Multiple convictions charged in two indictments or two accusations, or one indictment and one accusation filed in the same court prior to entry of judgment under any of them, shall be deemed to be one conviction. Convictions of crimes entered more than 10 years prior to an application for a certificate under N.J.S.A. 2A:168A-7 shall not be considered in determining whether a person has one criminal conviction.

§ 10A:71-9.3 Eligibility

(a) A certificate may be issued by the Board pursuant to N.J.S.A. 2A:168A-7 in regard to a qualified offender who is, or had previously been, under supervision by the Board if the Board determines pursuant to N.J.S.A. 2A:168A-8(b) that:

1. The applicant is convicted of a second, third or fourth degree offense and is eligible for relief as defined in (b) below;

2. The applicant has not been convicted of a crime since the conviction for which he or she is under supervision, has no pending criminal charge, and there is no information presented that such a charge is imminent;

3. Issuing the certificate will not pose a substantial risk to public safety; and

4. Issuing the certificate will assist in the successful reintegration of the offender and is consistent with the public interest.

(b) Pursuant to N.J.S.A. 2A:168A-8(c), a qualified offender is eligible for relief under (a) above if the offender has not been convicted of:

1. A first degree crime;

2. An offense to which N.J.S.A. 2C:43-7.2 applies;

3. A second degree offense defined in Chapters 13, 14, 15, 16, 24, 27, 30, 33 or 38 of Title 2C of the New Jersey Statutes;

4. A violation of N.J.S.A. 2C:24-4a. or N.J.S.A. 2C:24-4b.(4);

5. A crime requiring registration pursuant to N.J.S.A. 2C:7-2;

6. A crime committed against a public entity or against a public officer;

7. A crime enumerated in N.J.S.A. 43:1-3.1, committed by a public employee, which involves or touches upon the employee's office,

position or employment, such that the crime was related directly to the person's performance in, or circumstances flowing from, the specific public office or employment held by the person;

8. Any crime committed against a person 16 years of age or younger, or a disabled or handicapped person; or

9. A conspiracy or attempt to commit any of the crimes described in this subsection.

(c) The Board may issue a certificate in regard to a qualified offender, when three years have passed since the applicant has completed the parole supervision portion of his or her sentence and the Board determines pursuant to N.J.S.A. 2A:168A-8(d) that:

1. The applicant is eligible for relief as defined in (d) below;

2. Issuing the certificate does not pose a substantial risk to public safety; and

3. Issuing the certificate will assist in the successful reintegration of the offender and is consistent with the public interest.

(d) Pursuant to N.J.S.A. 2A:168A-8(e), a qualified offender is eligible for relief under (c) above if he or she has remained without criminal involvement since his or her conviction, including that he or she has not subsequently been convicted of a crime, has no pending charges for any crime and there is no information presented that such a charge is imminent; and is applying for relief from a conviction other than:

1. A first degree crime;

2. Any of the offenses to which N.J.S.A. 2C:43-7.2 applies;

3. A violation of N.J.S.A. 2C:24-4a. or N.J.S.A. 2C:24-4b.(4);

4. A crime requiring registration pursuant to N.J.S.A. 2C:7-2;

5. A crime enumerated in N.J.S.A. 43:1-3.1, committed by a public employee, which involves or touches upon the employee's office, position or employment, such that the crime was related directly to the person's performance in, or circumstances flowing from, the specific public office or employment held by the person;

6. A crime committed against a person 16 years of age or younger, or a disabled or handicapped person; or

7. A conspiracy or attempt to commit any offense described in this subsection.

(e) The certificate issued pursuant to (a) or (c) above may suspend disabilities, forfeitures and bars generally within the limits of N.J.S.A. 2A:168A-7 et seq., or only certain disabilities, forfeitures and bars specifically named in the certificate document issued by the Board.

§ 10A:71-9.4 Presumption of rehabilitation

Pursuant to N.J.S.A. 2A:168A-9, a certificate issued pursuant to N.J.S.A. 2A:168A-7 shall be presumptive evidence of the subject's rehabilitation when considered in regard to public employment as defined in N.J.S.A. 2A:168A-7 and N.J.A.C. 10A:71-9.2, or in conjunction with any licensing, or certification process to which this act applies, which in any particular case may or may not be overcome by other evidence or information. A certificate granted under N.J.S.A. 2A:168A-7 shall not prevent any judicial, administrative, licensing or other body, board, authority or public official from relying on grounds other than the fact of the criminal conviction in exercising any discretionary authority, if any, to suspend, revoke, refuse to issue or refuse to renew any license, permit or other authority or privilege or to determine eligibility or suitability for employment.

§ 10A:71-9.5 Procedure

(a) The applicant shall apply to the Board for a certificate on forms prescribed and furnished by the Board.

(b) Upon receipt of the application, the Board may initiate a confidential investigation, which shall contain all pertinent information, with particular reference to the need the applicant has for the use he or she expects to make of the certificate.

(c) The applicant shall be required to furnish all documentary evidence required by the Board.

§ 10A:71-9.6 Notification

(a) The Board shall provide written notice to the appropriate prosecutor of the pendency of an application submitted pursuant to this subchapter within 30 days of receipt of the application.

(b) The Board shall provide written notice to the appropriate prosecutor of the decision rendered by the Board on an application submitted pursuant to this subchapter within 30 days of the date of the decision.

(c) The Board shall provide written notice to the applicant of its decision within 30 days of the date of the decision.

(d) The original copy of the certificate, if granted, shall be filed with the Secretary of State.

(e) A copy of the certificate, if granted, shall be provided to the applicant.

(f) The certificate document provided to the applicant shall include a statement that the document is a copy and that a certifying authority, licensing authority or public employer should confirm with the Secretary of State that the certificate remains valid.

(g) If the Board should revoke a certificate pursuant to N.J.A.C. 10A:71-9.7, the Board shall provide written notice to the person who is the subject of the certificate, the appropriate prosecutor, the Secretary of State, the appropriate certifying authority, licensing authority or public employer within 15 days of the date of decision.

§ 10A:71-9.7 Revocation of certificate

(a) In accordance with N.J.S.A. 2A:168A-11, a certificate granted pursuant to N.J.S.A. 2A:168A-7 shall no longer be valid if the person who is the subject of the certificate is indicted for a first or second degree crime or convicted of a crime.

(b) Upon presentation of satisfactory proof that the criminal charges or indictment have been dismissed, or of an acquittal after trial, a certificate revoked under the circumstances described in (a) above may be reinstated by the Board.

(c) A certificate may be revoked at any time upon application of the prosecutor or on the Board's own initiative when information is received that circumstances have materially changed, such that the relief would not be authorized under N.J.S.A. 2A:168A-7 et seq., or is no longer in the public interest.

(d) A person who is the subject of a certificate shall be provided written notice prior to the Board rendering a decision to revoke the certificate. The person who is the subject of the certificate may provide a written statement for consideration by the Board as to why the certificate should not be revoked. The written statement must be received by the Board within 21 days of the person who is the subject of a certificate receiving the Board's notice. If a written statement is not received within the specified time period, the Board may proceed to consider the matter.

(e) The notice provided pursuant to (d) above shall not be required if the basis for revocation of the certificate is an indictment for a first or second degree crime or the conviction for the commission of a crime.

(f) Upon notice of the decision by the Board to revoke a certificate, the person who is the subject of the certificate shall surrender the certificate to the Board.

§ 10A:71-9.8 Board action

A decision by the Board to grant or revoke a certificate shall be rendered pursuant to N.J.A.C. 10A:71-1.2(h) and (i).

APPENDIX J

Expungement Forms (A-G)

Petition for Expungement
(Form A)

_____
(your name)

_____
(your address)

_____
(city, state, zip code)

_____
(your telephone number)

_____
(your social security number)

Superior Court of New Jersey
Law Division
County _____
(where you are filing)

Docket No. _____
(clerk will fill in)

Appearing Pro Se

In the Matter of the Expungement of the
Criminal/Juvenile Records of

_____
(your name)

Civil Action

Petition for Expungement

I, _____, residing at _____
(your name)   (address)

_____ SAY.
(address - continued)

1. My date of birth is _____.

2. I was arrested/taken into custody on _____, in _____ N.J.
    (municipality)

    and charged with _____, in
    (name of offense)

    violation of *N.J.S.A.* _____.
    (statute)

3. The original Indictment/Accusation/Summons/Warrant/Complaint/Docket number was

    _____.

*4. On _____, the charge of _____
    (name of offense)

    was dismissed by _____ after conditional discharge, pretrial
    (name of court)

    intervention program, juvenile conference committee, intake service conference or

    deferred disposition was successfully completed.

> * If you did not have a conditional discharge, pretrial intervention, juvenile conference committee, intake
> service conference or deferred disposition, cross out "after conditional discharge, pretrial intervention
> program, juvenile conference committee, intake service conference or deferred disposition was
> successfully completed." **If you were convicted or adjudicated delinquent of the offense described
> above, cross out paragraph 4 completely.**

Kit Revised: 04/2009, CN 10557 (How to Expunge Your Criminal and/or Juvenile Record)   page 12 of 34
Form Revised: 04/2009, CN 10171 (Petition for Expungement)

283

Petition for Expungement
(Form A - Continued)

*5. On _____ , I was found guilty / adjudicated delinquent of the charge of

_____ , in violation of *N.J.S.A.* _____
(name of offense)   (statute)

and was sentenced to _____ .

I completed jail/prison/ incarceration time on _____ ; probation on _____
and I paid the fine on _____

> * If you were not found guilty or adjudicated delinquent, cross out paragraph 5 completely.
> If you were not sentenced to jail/prison time/incarceration, probation, or a fine, write "n/a" (not applicable) in the appropriate spaces.

If you have no other arrests, cross out numbers 6 through 13.

6. I was arrested/ taken into custody on _____ , in _____ , N.J.
   (municipality)

   and charged with _____ , in
   (name of offense)

   violation of *N.J.S.A.* _____ .
   (statute)

7. The original Indictment/Accusation/Summons/Warrant/Complaint/Docket number was

   _____ .

*8. On _____ , the charge of _____
   (name of offense)

   was dismissed by _____ after conditional discharge, pretrial
   (name of court)

   intervention program, juvenile conference committee, intake service conference or

   deferred disposition was successfully completed.

> * If you did not have a conditional discharge, pretrial intervention program, juvenile conference committee, intake service conference or deferred disposition, cross out "after conditional discharge, pretrial intervention program, juvenile conference committee, intake service conference or deferred disposition was successfully completed."
> **If you were convicted or adjudicated delinquent of the offense described above, cross out paragraph 8 completely.**

Kit Revised: 04/2009, CN 10557 (How to Expunge Your Criminal and/or Juvenile Record)   page 13 of 34
Form Revised: 04/2009, CN 10171 (Petition for Expungement)

284

Petition for Expungement
(Form A - Continued)

*9. On _____, I was found guilty / adjudicated delinquent of the charge of

_____, in violation of *N.J.S.A.* _____
(name of offense)   (statute)

and was sentenced to _____.

I completed jail/prison/ incarceration time on _____; probation on _____
and I paid the fine on _____

> * If you were not found guilty or adjudicated delinquent, cross out paragraph 9 completely.
> If you were not sentenced to jail/prison/incarceration time, probation, or a fine, write "n/a" (not applicable) in the appropriate spaces.

If you have no other arrests, cross out numbers 10 through 13.

10. I was arrested/ taken into custody on _____, in _____ N.J.
(municipality)

and charged with _____, in
(name of offense)

violation of *N.J.S.A.* _____.
(statute)

11. The original Indictment/Accusation/Summons/Warrant/Complaint/Docket number was

_____.

*12. On _____, the charge of _____
(name of offense)

was dismissed by _____ after conditional discharge, pretrial
(name of court)

intervention program, juvenile conference committee, intake service conference or

deferred disposition was successfully completed.

> * If you did not have a conditional discharge, pretrial intervention program, juvenile conference committee, intake service conference or deferred disposition, cross out "after conditional discharge, pretrial intervention program, juvenile conference committee, intake service conference or deferred disposition was successfully completed."
> **If you were convicted or adjudicated delinquent of the offense described above, cross out paragraph 12 completely.**

Kit Revised: 04/2009, CN 10557 (How to Expunge Your Criminal and/or Juvenile Record)   page 14 of 34
Form Revised: 04/2009, CN 10171 (Petition for Expungement)

285

Petition for Expungement
(Form A - Continued)

*13. On _____ , I was found guilty / adjudicated delinquent of the charge of

_____ , in violation of *N.J.S.A.* _____
            (name of offense)   (statute)

and was sentenced to _____ .

I completed jail/prison/ incarceration time on _____ ; probation on _____
and I paid the fine on _____

> * If you were not found guilty or adjudicated delinquent, cross out paragraph 13 completely.
> If you were not sentenced to jail/prison/incarceration time, probation, or a fine, write "n/a" (not applicable) in the appropriate spaces.

NOTE: **If you have additional arrests as an adult or were taken into custody as a juvenile by the police, you must re-draft this entire petition and include those arrests in the same form as this petition.**

14.   I request that this Court grant me an Expungement Order as authorized by *N.J.S.A.* 2C:52-1, *et seq.,* directing the Clerk of the Court and all relevant criminal/juvenile justice and law enforcement services of the State of New Jersey to expunge from their records all evidence of the arrest/conviction/disposition (police record of when you were taken into custody as a juvenile/adjudication of delinquency/disposition) and all proceedings in this matter, and further directing any New Jersey law enforcement agency which sent records of the adult arrest/juvenile custody and proceedings to the Federal Bureau of Investigation or any other law enforcement agency outside of New Jersey to inform the recipient and the agencies designated to retain control of expunged records to take sufficient precautions to ensure that such records and information are not released.

Respectfully submitted,

Signed: _____
                                (your signature)

               _____
                             (your name printed)

Kit Revised: 04/2009, CN 10557 (How to Expunge Your Criminal and/or Juvenile Record)   page 15 of 34
Form Revised: 04/2009, CN 10171 (Petition for Expungement)

286

Verification
(Form A - Continued)

_____ , of full age, being duly sworn
(Your Name)

according to law, upon his oath deposes and says:

1. I am the Petitioner in this matter and statements made in this Petition are true to the best of my knowledge.

2. There are no disorderly persons, petty disorderly persons, or indictable charges pending against me at this time.

3. I am seeking expungement of a conviction on a criminal case and I have never been granted an expungement of an indictable conviction by any state or federal court. **(If you are not seeking expungement of an indictable offense, cross out #3.)**

Signed: _____
(your signature before a Notary)

_____
(your name printed)

Sworn to and subscribed before me this
_____ day of _____, _____

_____
(Notary's signature)

Kit Revised: 04/2009, CN 10557 (How to Expunge Your Criminal and/or Juvenile Record)   page 16 of 34
Form Revised: 04/2009, CN 10171 (Petition for Expungement)

287

ORDER FOR HEARING
(Form B)

Superior Court of New Jersey
Law Division
County _____
_____ (where you are filing)
(your name)

Docket No. _____
_____ (clerk will fill in)
(your address)

_____
(city, state, zip code)

Appearing Pro Se

In the Matter of the Expungement of the Criminal/Juvenile Records of
_____
(your name)

Civil Action

Order for Hearing

This matter having been opened to the Court upon the annexed Petition of
_____, and for good cause appearing;
(your name)

IT IS ORDERED this _____ day of _____, _____, that a
Hearing before this Court is set for the _____ day of _____, _____
at _____ o'clock _____.m. to determine whether an Order of Expungement shall be granted;

IT IS FURTHER ORDERED that Petitioner shall send by certified mail, copies of this Order
and Petition to the following officials within five (5) days of this Order:

The Attorney General of New Jersey

The Superintendent of the New Jersey State Police, Expungement Unit

The Prosecutor of _____ County

Clerk(s) of the _____ Municipal Court(s),

Chief(s) of the _____ Police Department(s),

Chief of the _____ County Probation Department

The Warden of the _____ Jail/Prison

The Superintendent of _____ (for juveniles only)

_____ County Family Division

The Division of Criminal Justice, Records and Identification Unit

_____
Judge, Superior Court of New Jersey

Kit Revised: 04/2009, CN 10557 (How to Expunge Your Criminal and/or Juvenile Record)   page 18 of 34
Form Revised: 04/2009, CN 10172 (Order for Hearing)

288

Expungement Order
(Form C)

_____
(your name)

_____
(your address)

_____
(city, state, zip code)

Appearing Pro Se

```
In the Matter of the Expungement of the
Criminal/Juvenile Records of

_____
            (your name)
```

Superior Court of New Jersey
Law Division
County _____
(where you are filing)

Docket No. _____
(clerk will fill in)

Civil Action

Expungement Order

This matter having been opened to the Court upon the Verified Petition of

_____ whose date of birth is _____ and
(your name)   (birth date)

social security number is _____, and it appearing that the requirements for
(your social security number)

Expungement under _N.J.S.A._ 2C:52-1, et seq. have been satisfied;

IT IS ORDERED this _____ day of _____, _____, that the

The Attorney General of New Jersey

The Superintendent of the New Jersey State Police, Expungement Unit

The Prosecutor of _____ County

Clerk(s) of the _____ Municipal Court(s),

Chief(s) of the _____ Police Department(s),

Chief of the _____ County Probation Department

The Warden of the _____ Jail/Prison

The Superintendent of _____ (for juveniles only)

Deputy Clerk of the Superior Court of New Jersey, _____ County, remove

from their records all information relating to

_____'s
(your name)

(1) _____ arrest/custody on the charge of violating _N.J.S.A._ _____;
(date of arrest)   (statute)

(2) _____ arrest/custody on the charge of violating _N.J.S.A._ _____;
(date of arrest)   (statute)

(3) _____ arrest/custody on the charge of violating _N.J.S.A._ _____;
(date of arrest)   (statute)

Kit Revised: 04/2009, CN 10557 (How to Expunge Your Criminal and/or Juvenile Record)   page 20 of 34
Form Revised: 04/2009, CN 10173 (Expungement Order)

289

EXPUNGEMENT ORDER
(Form C – Continued)

and remove all records concerning the subsequent criminal and/or juvenile proceedings regarding such charge(s), including any conviction(s), adjudication(s) of delinquency or disposition(s), if applicable, and place such information in the control of a person within the office designated to retain control over expunged records.

IT IS FURTHER ORDERED that any of the above officers or agencies which sent fingerprints and/or any records of the above arrest/conviction/adjudication/disposition and proceedings to the Federal Bureau of Investigation or any other office or agency shall notify same of this Order and that the agencies designated to retain such records take sufficient precautions to insure that such records and information are not released.

IT IS FURTHER ORDERED that any records, or the information therein, shall not be released except as provided under the provision of *N.J.S.A.* 2C:52-1, *et seq.* and that the persons designated to retain control over expunged records take sufficient precautions to insure that such records and information are not released.

IT IS FURTHER ORDERED that in response to requests for information or records, the court office or law enforcement agency shall reply with respect to the arrest/conviction/adjudication/disposition, which is the subject of this Order, that there is no record.

IT IS FURTHER ORDERED that the arrest/conviction/adjudication/disposition, which is the subject of this Order, shall be deemed, in contemplation of law, not to have occurred, and the Petitioner may answer accordingly any question relating to this occurrence except as provided in *N.J.S.A.* 2C:52-27.

IT IS FURTHER ORDERED that this Order does not expunge the records contained in the Controlled Dangerous Substances Registry created pursuant to *P.L.* 1970, c. 227 (C.26:2G-17 et seq.) or the registry created by the Administrative Office of the Courts pursuant to *N.J.S.A.* 2C:43-21.

_____
Judge, Superior Court of New Jersey

Kit Revised: 04/2009, CN 10557 (How to Expunge Your Criminal and/or Juvenile Record)   page 21 of 34
Form Revised: 04/2009, CN 10173 (Expungement Order)

290

Cover Letter to Court When Filing Papers
(Form D)

_____
(date)

Clerk, Superior Court of New Jersey

_____
(county)

_____
(address)

_____
(city, state, zip code)

Re: In the Matter of the Expungement of the Criminal/Juvenile Records of:

_____
(your name)

Dear Sir or Madam:

Enclosed are an original and two copies of a _Petition, Order for Hearing_ and _Proposed Final Order_ in this matter. Kindly submit them to the appropriate Judge and return copies marked "Filed."

Thank you.

                        Sincerely,

                        _____
                                 (your signature)

                        _____
                                 (your name)

                        _____
                                 (address)

                        _____
                             (city, state, zip code)

Enc:

Kit Revised: 04/2009, CN 10557 (How to Expunge Your Criminal and/or Juvenile Record)   page 23 of 34
Form Revised: 04/2009, CN 10174 (Cover Letter to Court When Filing Papers)

291

Cover Letter
(Form E)

_____
(date)

Attorney General, State of New Jersey Hughes Justice Complex Post Office Box 080 Trenton, NJ 08625	Superintendent, State Police Expungement Unit Post Office Box 7068 West Trenton, NJ 08628
Prosecutor, _____ _____ (address) _____ (city, state, zip code)	Municipal Court Clerk _____ _____ (address) _____ (city, state, zip code)
Chief of Police, _____ _____ (address) _____ (city, state, zip code)	Warden/Jail _____ (name of jail/prison) _____ (address) _____ (city, state, zip code)
County Probation Office _____ _____ (address) _____ (city, state, zip code)	Superintendent _____ (name of place of incarceration) _____ (address) _____ (city, state, zip code)
County Sheriff, _____ _____ (address) _____ (city, state, zip code)	Division of Criminal Justice Records and Identification Unit 25 Market Street Post Office Box 085 Trenton, New Jersey 08625
County Family Division _____ _____ (address) _____ (city, state, zip code)	

Re: Expungement Hearing: _____ at _____ Docket No. _____
(date)   (time)

Dear Sir or Madam:

Enclosed are copies of the Petition for Expungement, Order for Hearing, and proposed Final Order in this matter.

Sincerely,

_____
(your signature)

_____
(your name)

_____
(address)

_____
(city, state, zip code)

Certified Mail No. _____

Kit Revised: 04/2009, CN 10557 (How to Expunge Your Criminal and/or Juvenile Record)   page 25 of 34
Form Revised: 04/2009, CN 10175 (Cover Letter)

292

Proof of Notice
(Form F)

_____
(your name)

_____
(your address)

_____
(city, state, zip code)

Superior Court of New Jersey
Law Division
County _____
(where you are filing)

Docket No. _____
(fill in docket number)

Appearing Pro Se

In the Matter of the Expungement of the Criminal/Juvenile Records of
_____
(your name)

Civil Action

Proof of Notice

On _____, I mailed a copy of the Petition for Expungement, Order for Hearing
(date)
and Proposed Final Order by way of certified mail, return receipt requested to the following:

The Attorney General of New Jersey

The Superintendent of the New Jersey State Police, Expungement Unit

The Prosecutor of _____ County

Chief(s) of the _____ Police Department(s)

Clerk(s) of the _____ Municipal Court(s)

The Warden of the _____ Jail/Prison

The Superintendent of _____ (for juveniles only)

The _____ County Probation Division

The Division of Criminal Justice, Records and Identification Unit

Enclosed are the certified mail receipts that were returned to me.

_____
(your signature)

_____
(date)

Kit Revised: 04/2009, CN 10557 (How to Expunge Your Criminal and/or Juvenile Record)
Form Revised: 04/2009, CN 10176 (Proof of Notice)

page 27 of 34

293

Cover Letter
(Form G)

_____
(date)

Attorney General, State of New Jersey Hughes Justice Complex Post Office Box 080 Trenton, NJ 08625	Superintendent, State Police Expungement Unit Post Office Box 7068 West Trenton, NJ 08628
Prosecutor, _____ _____ (address) _____ (city, state, zip code)	Municipal Court Clerk _____ _____ (address) _____ (city, state, zip code)
Chief of Police,_____ _____ (address) _____ (city, state, zip code)	Warden/Jail _____ (name of jail/prison) _____ (address) _____ (city, state, zip code)
County Probation Office_____ _____ (address) _____ (city, state, zip code)	Superintendent _____ (name of place of incarceration) _____ (address) _____ (city, state, zip code)
County Identification Bureau, _____ (address) _____ (city, state, zip code)	Division of Criminal Justice Records and Identification Unit 25 Market Street Post Office Box 085 Trenton, New Jersey 08625
County Family Division _____ _____ (address) _____ (city, state, zip code)	

Re: In the Matter of the Expungement of the Criminal/Juvenile Records of

_____   _____
(your name)   (docket no.)

Dear Sir or Madam:

Enclosed is a copy of an Expungement Order. Please take the appropriate action to see that these records are expunged.

Sincerely,

_____
(your signature)

_____
(your name)

_____
(address)

_____
(city, state, zip code)

Certified Mail No. _____

Kit Revised: 04/2009, CN 10557 (How to Expunge Your Criminal and/or Juvenile Record)   page 29 of 34
Form Revised: 04/2009, CN 10177 (Cover Letter)

294

Petition for Expungement
(Form A)

[full name]
[address]
[city state zip code]
[telephone number]
[social security]
Appearing Pro Se

Superior Court of New Jersey
Law Division
[county]

Docket No:

In the Matter of Expungement
of the Criminal /Juvenile Records of

Civil Action

Verified Petition

For Expungement

[full name]

_____

Petitioner, [full name] residing at [address] [city state zip code], by way of verified

Petition does say:

GENERAL RECITATION

1.   The petitioner's date of birth is [date of birth].

COUNT ONE

2.   On [date of arrest 1], Petitioner was arrested/taken into custody in [city of

arrest 1], N.J. by the [agency who arrested 1] and charged with a violation of N.J.S.A.

[statute of arrest 1], [name of arrest 1].

3.   The original Indictment/Summons/Warrant/Complaint/Docket number was

[Indictment number arrest 1].

4.   On [date completed diversion arrest 1], the charge of [name of arrest 1]

was dismissed by [name of court arrest 1].

Petitioner successfully completed a [diversion for arrest 1], on [date diversion completed arrest 1].

5.   Petitioner was found guilty / adjudicated delinquent of [name of arrest 1] in violation of N.J.S.A. [statute of arrest 1] and was sentenced to [sentence for arrest 1]. Petitioner completed jail/prison/incarceration time on [date completed jail 1]. Petitioner completed probation on [date completed probation arrest 1]. Petitioner received fines and penalties totaling [amount fines arrest 1]. Petitioner paid the fines in full on [date paid fine arrest 1].

COUNT TWO

6.   On [date of arrest 2], Petitioner was arrested in [city of arrest 2] by the [agency who arrested 2] and charged with a violation of N.J.S.A. [statute of arrest 2], [name of arrest 2].

7.   The original Indictment/Summons/Warrant/Complaint/Docket number was [Indictment number arrest 2].

8.   On [date completed diversion arrest 2], the charge of [name of arrest 2] was dismissed by [name of court arrest 2]. Petitioner successfully completed a [diversion for arrest 2], on [date diversion completed arrest 2].

9.   Petitioner was found guilty / adjudicated delinquent of [name of arrest 2] in violation of N.J.S.A. [statute of arrest 2] and was sentenced to [sentence for arrest 2]. Petitioner completed jail/prison/incarceration time on [date completed jail 2]. Petitioner completed probation on [date completed probation arrest 2]. Petitioner received fines and penalties totaling [amount fines arrest 2]. Petitioner paid

the fines in full on [date paid fine arrest 2].

COUNT THREE

6.   On [date of arrest 3], Petitioner was arrested in [city of arrest 3] by the [agency who arrested 3] and charged with a violation of N.J.S.A. [statute of arrest 3], [name of arrest 3].

7.   The original Indictment/Summons/Warrant/Complaint/Docket number was [Indictment number arrest 3].

8.   On [date completed diversion arrest 3], the charge of [name of arrest 3] was dismissed by [name of court arrest 3]. Petitioner successfully completed a [diversion for arrest 3], on [date diversion completed arrest 3].

9.   Petitioner was found guilty / adjudicated delinquent of [name of arrest 3] in violation of N.J.S.A. [statute of arrest 3] and was sentenced to [sentence for arrest 3]. Petitioner completed jail/prison/incarceration time on [date completed jail 3]. Petitioner completed probation on [date completed probation arrest 3]. Petitioner received fines and penalties totaling [amount fines arrest 3]. Petitioner paid the fines in full on [date paid fine arrest 3].

COUNT FOUR

6.   On [date of arrest 4], Petitioner was arrested in [city of arrest 4] by the [agency who arrested 4] and charged with a violation of N.J.S.A. [statute of arrest 4], [name of arrest 4].

7.   The original Indictment/Summons/Warrant/Complaint/Docket number was [Indictment number arrest 4].

8.   On [date completed diversion arrest 4], the charge of [name of arrest 4]

was dismissed by [name of court arrest 4]. Petitioner successfully completed a [diversion for arrest 4], on [date diversion completed arrest 4].

9.   Petitioner was found guilty / adjudicated delinquent of [name of arrest 4] in violation of N.J.S.A. [statute of arrest 4] and was sentenced to [sentence for arrest 4]. Petitioner completed jail/prison/incarceration time on [date completed jail 4]. Petitioner completed probation on [date completed probation arrest 4]. Petitioner received fines and penalties totaling [amount fines arrest 4]. Petitioner paid the fines in full on [date paid fine arrest 4].

COUNT FIVE

6.   On [date of arrest 5], Petitioner was arrested in [city of arrest 5] by the [agency who arrested 5] and charged with a violation of N.J.S.A. [statute of arrest 5], [name of arrest 5].

7.   The original Indictment/Summons/Warrant/Complaint/Docket number was [Indictment number arrest 5].

8.   On [date completed diversion arrest 5], the charge of [name of arrest 5] was dismissed by [name of court arrest 5]. Petitioner successfully completed a [diversion for arrest 5], on [date diversion completed arrest 5].

9.   Petitioner was found guilty / adjudicated delinquent of [name of arrest 5] in violation of N.J.S.A. [statute of arrest 5] and was sentenced to [sentence for arrest 5]. Petitioner completed jail/prison/incarceration time on [date completed jail 5]. Petitioner completed probation on [date completed probation arrest 5]. Petitioner received fines and penalties totaling [amount fines arrest 5]. Petitioner paid the fines in full on [date paid fine arrest 5].

COUNT SIX

6.   On [date of arrest 6], Petitioner was arrested in [city of arrest 6] by the [agency who arrested 6] and charged with a violation of N.J.S.A. [statute of arrest 6], [name of arrest 6].

7.   The original Indictment/Summons/Warrant/Complaint/Docket number was [Indictment number arrest 6].

8.   On [date completed diversion arrest 6], the charge of [name of arrest 6] was dismissed by [name of court arrest 6]. Petitioner successfully completed a [diversion for arrest 6], on [date diversion completed arrest 6].

9.   Petitioner was found guilty / adjudicated delinquent of [name of arrest 6] in violation of N.J.S.A. [statute of arrest 6] and was sentenced to [sentence for arrest 6]. Petitioner completed jail/prison/incarceration time on [date completed jail 6]. Petitioner completed probation on [date completed probation arrest 6]. Petitioner received fines and penalties totaling [amount fines arrest 6]. Petitioner paid the fines in full on [date paid fine arrest 6].

COUNT SEVEN

6.   On [date of arrest 7], Petitioner was arrested in [city of arrest 7] by the [agency who arrested 7] and charged with a violation of N.J.S.A. [statute of arrest 7], [name of arrest 7].

7.   The original Indictment/Summons/Warrant/Complaint/Docket number was [Indictment number arrest 7].

8.   On [date completed diversion arrest 7], the charge of [name of arrest 7] was dismissed by [name of court arrest 7]. Petitioner successfully completed a

[diversion for arrest 7], on [date diversion completed arrest 7].

9.   Petitioner was found guilty / adjudicated delinquent of [name of arrest 7] in violation of N.J.S.A. [statute of arrest 7] and was sentenced to [sentence for arrest 7]. Petitioner completed jail/prison/incarceration time on [date completed jail 7]. Petitioner completed probation on [date completed probation arrest 7]. Petitioner received fines and penalties totaling [amount fines arrest 7]. Petitioner paid the fines in full on [date paid fine arrest 7].

COUNT EIGHT

6.   On [date of arrest 8], Petitioner was arrested in [city of arrest 8] by the [agency who arrested 8] and charged with a violation of N.J.S.A. [statute of arrest 8], [name of arrest 8].

7.   The original Indictment/Summons/Warrant/Complaint/Docket number was [Indictment number arrest 8].

8.   On [date completed diversion arrest 8], the charge of [name of arrest 8] was dismissed by [name of court arrest 8]. Petitioner successfully completed a [diversion for arrest 8], on [date diversion completed arrest 8].

9.   Petitioner was found guilty / adjudicated delinquent of [name of arrest 8] in violation of N.J.S.A. [statute of arrest 8] and was sentenced to [sentence for arrest 8]. Petitioner completed jail/prison/incarceration time on [date completed jail 8]. Petitioner completed probation on [date completed probation arrest 8]. Petitioner received fines and penalties totaling [amount fines arrest 8]. Petitioner paid the fines in full on [date paid fine arrest 8].

10.   Since the date of the aforementioned charges and dismissal of same, no

subsequent convictions for any offense were entered against the petitioner.

Wherefore, Petitioner respectfully requests that this Court grant me an Expungement Order as authorized by N.J.S.A. 2C:52-1, et seq., directing the Clerk of the Court and all relevant criminal/juvenile justice and law enforcement services of the State of New Jersey to expunge from their records all evidence of the arrest/conviction/disposition (police record of when you were taken into custody as a juvenile/adjudication of delinquency/disposition) and all proceedings in this matter, and further directing any New Jersey law enforcement agency which sent records of the adult arrest/juvenile custody and proceedings to the Federal Bureau of Investigation or any other law enforcement agency outside of New Jersey to inform the recipient and the agencies designated to retain control of expunged records to take sufficient precautions to ensure that such records and information are not released.

ADDITIONAL ARRESTS

11.   On [date of arrest add 1], Petitioner was arrested in [city of arrest add 1], [state of arrest add 1] by the [agency who arrested add 1] and charged with a violation of [statute of arrest add 1], [name of arrest add 1].

The original Indictment/Summons/Warrant/Complaint/Docket number was [Indictment number arrest add 1].

On [date completed diversion arrest add 1], the charge of [name of arrest add 1] was dismissed by [name of court arrest add 1].

Petitioner successfully completed a [diversion for arrest add 1], on [date diversion completed arrest add 1].

Petitioner was found guilty / adjudicated delinquent of [name of arrest add 1] in violation of N.J.S.A. [statute of arrest add 1] and was sentenced to

[sentence for arrest add 1].

Petitioner completed jail/prison/incarceration time on [date completed jail add 1].

Petitioner completed probation on [date completed probation arrest add 1].

Petitioner received fines and penalties totaling [amount fines arrest add 1]. Petitioner

paid the fines in full on [date paid fine arrest add 1].

Petitioner does not seek expungement of this charge.

Petitioner recites this offense solely for the purposes of completeness.

11.   On [date of arrest add 2], Petitioner was arrested in [city of arrest add

2], [state of arrest add 2] by the [agency who arrested add 2] and charged with a

violation of [statute of arrest add 2], [name of arrest add 2].

The original Indictment/Summons/Warrant/Complaint/Docket number was

[Indictment number arrest add 2].

On [date completed diversion arrest add 2], the charge of [name of arrest

add 2] was dismissed by [name of court arrest add 2].

Petitioner successfully completed a [diversion for arrest add 2], on [date diversion

completed arrest add 2].

Petitioner was found guilty / adjudicated delinquent of [name of arrest

add 2] in violation of N.J.S.A. [statute of arrest add 2] and was sentenced to

[sentence for arrest add 2].

Petitioner completed jail/prison/incarceration time on [date completed jail add 2].

Petitioner completed probation on [date completed probation arrest add 2].

Petitioner received fines and penalties totaling [amount fines arrest add 2]. Petitioner paid the fines in full on [date paid fine arrest add 2].

Petitioner does not seek expungement of this charge.

Petitioner recites this offense solely for the purposes of completeness.

11. On [date of arrest add 3], Petitioner was arrested in [city of arrest add 3], [state of arrest add 3] by the [agency who arrested add 3] and charged with a violation of [statute of arrest add 3], [name of arrest add 3].

The original Indictment/Summons/Warrant/Complaint/Docket number was [Indictment number arrest add 3].

On [date completed diversion arrest add 3], the charge of [name of arrest add 3] was dismissed by [name of court arrest add 3].

Petitioner successfully completed a [diversion for arrest add 3], on [date diversion completed arrest add 3].

Petitioner was found guilty / adjudicated delinquent of [name of arrest add 3] in violation of N.J.S.A. [statute of arrest add 3] and was sentenced to [sentence for arrest add 3].

Petitioner completed jail/prison/incarceration time on [date completed jail add 3].

Petitioner completed probation on [date completed probation arrest add 3].

Petitioner received fines and penalties totaling [amount fines arrest add 3]. Petitioner paid the fines in full on [date paid fine arrest add 3].

Petitioner does not seek expungement of this charge.

Petitioner recites this offense solely for the purposes of completeness.

11. On [date of arrest add 4], Petitioner was arrested in [city of arrest add 4], [state of arrest add 4] by the [agency who arrested add 4] and charged with a

violation of [statute of arrest add 4], [name of arrest add 4].

The original Indictment/Summons/Warrant/Complaint/Docket number was [Indictment number arrest add 4].

On [date completed diversion arrest add 4], the charge of [name of arrest add 4] was dismissed by [name of court arrest add 4].

Petitioner successfully completed a [diversion for arrest add 4], on [date diversion completed arrest add 4].

Petitioner was found guilty / adjudicated delinquent of [name of arrest add 4] in violation of N.J.S.A. [statute of arrest add 4] and was sentenced to [sentence for arrest add 4].

Petitioner completed jail/prison/incarceration time on [date completed jail add 4].

Petitioner completed probation on [date completed probation arrest add 4].

Petitioner received fines and penalties totaling [amount fines arrest add 4]. Petitioner paid the fines in full on [date paid fine arrest add 4].

11.   On [date of arrest add 5], Petitioner was arrested in [city of arrest add 5], [state of arrest add 5] by the [agency who arrested add 5] and charged with a violation of [statute of arrest add 5], [name of arrest add 5].

The original Indictment/Summons/Warrant/Complaint/Docket number was [Indictment number arrest add 5].

On [date completed diversion arrest add 5], the charge of [name of arrest add 5] was dismissed by [name of court arrest add 5].

Petitioner successfully completed a [diversion for arrest add 5], on [date diversion completed arrest add 5].

Petitioner was found guilty / adjudicated delinquent of [name of arrest

add 5] in violation of N.J.S.A. [statute of arrest add 5] and was sentenced to

[sentence for arrest add 5].

Petitioner completed jail/prison/incarceration time on [date completed jail add 5].

Petitioner completed probation on [date completed probation arrest add 5].

Petitioner received fines and penalties totaling [amount fines arrest add 5]. Petitioner

paid the fines in full on [date paid fine arrest add 5].

      11.   On [date of arrest add 6], Petitioner was arrested in [city of arrest add

6], [state of arrest add 6] by the [agency who arrested add 6] and charged with a

violation of [statute of arrest add 6], [name of arrest add 6].

The original Indictment/Summons/Warrant/Complaint/Docket number was

[Indictment number arrest add 6].

On [date completed diversion arrest add 6], the charge of [name of arrest

add 6] was dismissed by [name of court arrest add 6].

Petitioner successfully completed a [diversion for arrest add 6], on [date diversion

completed arrest add 6].

Petitioner was found guilty / adjudicated delinquent of [name of arrest

add 6] in violation of N.J.S.A. [statute of arrest add 6] and was sentenced to

[sentence for arrest add 6].

Petitioner completed jail/prison/incarceration time on [date completed jail add 6].

Petitioner completed probation on [date completed probation arrest add 6].

Petitioner received fines and penalties totaling [amount fines arrest add 6]. Petitioner

paid the fines in full on [date paid fine arrest add 6].

11.   On [date of arrest add 7], Petitioner was arrested in [city of arrest add 7], [state of arrest add 7] by the [agency who arrested add 7] and charged with a violation of [statute of arrest add 7], [name of arrest add 7].

The original Indictment/Summons/Warrant/Complaint/Docket number was [Indictment number arrest add 7].

On [date completed diversion arrest add 7], the charge of [name of arrest add 7] was dismissed by [name of court arrest add 7].

Petitioner successfully completed a [diversion for arrest add 7], on [date diversion completed arrest add 7].

Petitioner was found guilty / adjudicated delinquent of [name of arrest add 7] in violation of N.J.S.A. [statute of arrest add 7] and was sentenced to [sentence for arrest add 7].

11.   On [date of arrest add 8], Petitioner was arrested in [city of arrest add 8], [state of arrest add 8] by the [agency who arrested add 8] and charged with a violation of [statute of arrest add 8], [name of arrest add 8].

The original Indictment/Summons/Warrant/Complaint/Docket number was [Indictment number arrest add 8].

On [date completed diversion arrest add 8], the charge of [name of arrest add 8] was dismissed by [name of court arrest add 8].

Petitioner successfully completed a [diversion for arrest add 8], on [date diversion completed arrest add 8].

Petitioner was found guilty / adjudicated delinquent of [name of arrest add 8] in violation of N.J.S.A. [statute of arrest add 8] and was sentenced to [sentence for arrest add 8].

12.   As an adult, Petitioner has never been arrested or charged with any disorderly persons, petty disorderly persons, or criminal offense, or violation of a municipal ordinance, in any jurisdiction whatsoever, except as set forth herein. As a juvenile, Petitioner has never been taken into custody or charged with any action which, had Petitioner been an adult, would have constituted a disorderly persons, petty disorderly persons, or criminal offense, or violation of a municipal ordinance, in any jurisdiction whatsoever, except as set forth herein.

Respectfully submitted,

Signed: _____
                  (your signature)
                  [full name]

Verification Form
(Form A - Continued)

[full name], of full age, being duly sworn according to law, upon oath deposes and says:

1.   I am Petitioner in this matter and statements made in this Petition are true to the best of my personal knowledge, information, and belief. The foregoing petition is made in good faith for the causes set forth therein.

2.   There are no disorderly persons, petty disorderly persons, or indictable charges pending against me at this time.

3.   I have never previously been granted an expungement, sealing, or similar relief for a criminal conviction by any court in this State or other state or any Federal court.

Signed: _____

(your signature before a Notary)
[full name]

Sworn to and subscribed before me this
_____ day of _____, _____

_____
(Notary's Signature)

ORDER FOR HEARING
(Form B)

[full name]
[address]
[city state zip code]
[telephone number]
[social security]
Appearing Pro Se

Superior Court of New Jersey
Law Division

[county]

Docket No:

In the Matter of Expungement
of the Criminal /Juvenile Records of

Civil Action

Order for Hearing

[full name]

THIS MATTER having been opened to the Court upon the annexed Petition of

[full name] and for good cause appearing;

IT IS ORDERED this [OrderHearingDte] day of [OrderHearingMth],

OrderHearingYr], that a Hearing before this Court is set for the [HearingDte] day of

[HearingMth], HearingYr] at [HearingTime] o'clock _____.m to determine whether an

Order of Expungement shall be granted;

IT IS FURTHER ORDERED that the Petitioner shall send by certified mail,

copies of this Order and Petition to the following officials within five (5) days of this

Order:

    The Attorney General of New Jersey
    The Superintendent of the New Jersey State Police
    [CntyPro 1] County Prosecutor
    Clerk of the [MuniCrtName 1] Municipal Court(s)
    Chief of the [PoliceName 1] Police Department(s)

Chief of the [ProbationName 1] County Probation Department
The Warden of the [WardPrisonName 1] Jail/Prison
The Superintendant of [SuperName 1]
[JuvyFamCntyName 1] County Family Division
The Division of Criminal Justice, Records and Identification Unit

EXPUNGEMENT ORDER
(Form C)

[full name]
[address]
[city state zip code]
[telephone number]
[social security]
Appearing Pro Se

Superior Court of New Jersey
Law Division
[county]

Docket No:

In the Matter of Expungement
of the Criminal /Juvenile Records of

Civil Action

Expungement Order

[full name]

_____

    THIS MATTER having been opened to the Court upon the Verified Petition of [full name], residing at [address] [city state zip code], whose date of birth is [date of birth] and social security number is [social security], and it appearing that the requirements for Expungement under N.J.S.A. 2C:52-11, et seq. have been satisfied;

    IT IS ORDERED this [OrderExpungeDtDay] day of ,[OrderExpungeDtMth], [OrderExpungeDtYr] that the

        The Attorney General of New Jersey
        The Superintendent of the New Jersey State Police
        [CntyPro 1] County Prosecutor
        Clerk of the [MuniCrtName 1] Municipal Court(s)
        Chief of the [PoliceName 1] Police Department(s)
        Chief of the [ProbationName 1] County Probation Department
        The Warden of the [WardPrisonName 1] Jail/Prison
        The Superintendant of [SuperName 1]
        [JuvyFamCntyName 1] County Family Division
        The Division of Criminal Justice, Records and Identification Unit,

remove from their records all information relating to [full name]'s [name of arrest 1] arrest/custody on [date of arrest 1] on the charge of violating N.J.S.A. [name of statute 1] and remove all records concerning the subsequent criminal and/or juvenile proceedings regarding such charge(s), including any conviction(s), adjudication(s) of delinquency or disposition(s), if applicable, and place such information in the control of a person within the office designated to retain control over expunged records.

IT IS FURTHER ORDERED that any of the above officers or agencies which sent fingerprints and/or any records of the above arrest /conviction / adjudication / disposition and proceedings to the Federal Bureau of Investigation or any other office or agency shall notify same of this Order and that the agencies designated to retain such records take sufficient precautions to insure that such records and information are not released.

IT IS FURTHER ORDERED that any records, or the information therein, shall not be released except as provided under the provision of N.J.S.A. 2C:52-1, et seq. and that the persons designated to retain control over expunged records take sufficient precautions to insure that such records and information are not released.

IT IS FURTHER ORDERED that in response to requests for information or records, the court office or law enforcement agency shall reply with respect to the arrest/conviction/adjudication/disposition, which is the subject of this Order, that there is no record.

IT IS FURTHER ORDERED that the arrest/conviction/adjudication/disposition, which is the subject of this Order, shall be deemed, in contemplation of law, not to have occurred, and the Petitioner may answer accordingly any question relating to this occurrence except as provided in N.J.S.A. 2C:52-27.

IT IS FURTHER ORDERED that this Order does not expunge the records

contained in the Controlled Dangerous Substances Registry created pursuant to P.L.

1970, c. 227 (C.26:2G-17 et seq.) or the registry created by the Administrative Office of

the Courts pursuant to N.J.S.A. 2C:43-21.

_____
The Honorable Judge, J.S.C.

Cover Letter
(Form D)

_____
(date)

Clerk, Superior Court of New Jersey
[county]
[countystreetaddress]
[countycitystatezip]
Re: In the Matter of the Expungement of the Criminal/Juvenile Records of:
       [full name]
Dear Sir or Madam:
Enclosed are an original and two copies of a Verified Petition, Order for Hearing and Proposed Final Order in this matter. Kindly submit them to the appropriate Judge and return copies marked "Filed."
Thank you.

Sincerely,

_____
[full name]
[address]
[city state zip code]
[telephone number]

Cover Letter
(Form E)

_____
(date)

Attorney General, State of New Jersey
Hughes Justice Complex
Post Office Box 080
Trenton, NJ 08625

Superintendant, State Police
Expungement Unit
Post Office Box 7068
West Trenton, NJ 08628

Prosecutor, [CntyPro 1]
[CntyProStrAddress 1]
[CntyProcitystatezip 1]

Municipal Court Clerk, [MuniCrtName 1]
[MuniCityNameStrAddress 1]
[MuniCityNamecitystatezip 1]

Chief of Police, [PoliceName 1]
[PoliceStrAddress 1]
[Policecitystatezip 1]

Warden/Jail [WardPrisonName 1]
[WardPrisonStrAddress 1]
[WardPrisoncitystatezip 1]

County Probation Office [ProbationName 1]
[ProbationNameStrAddress 1]
[ProbationNamecitystatezip 1]

Superintendant [SuperName 1]
[SuperNameStrAddress 1]
[SuperNamecitystatezip 1]

County Sheriff, [SheriffName 1]
[SheriffStrAddress 1]
[Sheriffcitystatezip 1]

Division of Criminal Justice
Records and Identification Unit
25 Market Street
Post Office Box 085
Trenton, New Jersey 08625

County Family Division [JuvyFamCntyName 1]
[JuvyFamCntyStr 1]
[JuvyFamCntycitystatezip 1]

Re: Expungement Hearing: _____ at _____ Docket No. _____
                                     (date)   (time)

Dear Sir or Madam:
Enclosed are copies of the Verified Petition for Expungement, Order for Hearing and Proposed
Final Order in this matter.

Sincerely,

_____
[full name]
[address]
[city state zip code]
[telephone number]

Certified Mail No. _____

Proof of Service
(Form F)

[full name]
[address]
[city state zip code]
[telephone number]
[social security]
Appearing Pro Se

Superior Court of New Jersey
Law Division
[county]

Docket No:

In the Matter of Expungement
of the Criminal /Juvenile Records of

Civil Action

Proof of Service

[full name]

_____

On _____, I mailed a copy of the Verified Petition, Order of

Hearing, and Proposed Final Order by way of certified mail, return receipt requested to

the following:

    The Attorney General of New Jersey
    The Superintendent of the New Jersey State Police
    [CntyPro 1] County Prosecutor
    Clerk of the [MuniCrtName 1] Municipal Court(s)
    Chief of the [PoliceName 1] Police Department(s)
    Chief of the [ProbationName 1] County Probation Department
    The Warden of the [WardPrisonName 1] Jail/Prison
    The Superintendant of [SuperName 1]
    [JuvyFamCntyName 1] County Family Division
    The Division of Criminal Justice, Records and Identification Unit

Enclosed are the certified mail receipts that were returned to me.

_____   _____

(your signature)   (date)

Cover Letter
(Form G)

_____
(date)

Attorney General, State of New Jersey
Hughes Justice Complex
Post Office Box 080
Trenton, NJ 08625

Superintendant, State Police
Expungement Unit
Post Office Box 7068
West Trenton, NJ 08628

Prosecutor, [CntyPro 1]
[CntyProStrAddress 1]
[CntyProcitystatezip 1]

Municipal Court Clerk, [MuniCrtName 1]
[MuniCityNameStrAddress 1]
[MuniCityNamecitystatezip 1]

Chief of Police, [PoliceName 1]
[PoliceStrAddress 1]
[Policecitystatezip 1]

Warden/Jail [WardPrisonName 1]
[WardPrisonStrAddress 1]
[WardPrisoncitystatezip 1]

County Probation Office [ProbationName 1]
[ProbationNameStrAddress 1]
[ProbationNamecitystatezip 1]

Superintendant [SuperName 1]
[SuperNameStrAddress 1]
[SuperNamecitystatezip 1]

County Sheriff, [SheriffName 1]
[SheriffStrAddress 1]
[Sheriffcitystatezip 1]

Division of Criminal Justice
Records and Identification Unit
25 Market Street
Post Office Box 085
Trenton, New Jersey 08625

County Family Division [JuvyFamCntyName 1]
[JuvyFamCntyStr 1]
[JuvyFamCntycitystatezip 1]

Re: Expungement Hearing: _____ at _____ Docket No. _____
                                              (date)   (time)

Dear Sir or Madam:

Enclosed are copies of the Verified Petition for Expungement, Order for Hearing, and Proposed
Final Order in this matter.

Sincerely,

_____
[full name]
[address]
[city state zip code]
[telephone number]

Certified Mail No. _____

Made in the USA
Middletown, DE
13 November 2015